Praise for
The Hum of Angels

"Books on the angelic in the Bible are usually of varying quality—so fluffy and story filled they lack a coherent basis in Scripture, or so impenetrably philosophical one can't apply them to the normal Christian life. Scot McKnight's *The Hum of Angels* carefully avoids all these pitfalls and presents a sound and balanced biblical vision of God's angelic realm and its work. He helpfully reimagines the ministry of angels, while keeping his work rooted in and framed by Scripture. *The Hum of Angels* is a worthy addition to the library of anyone wanting a solid, insightful, and scriptural view of God's angelic ministers."

> —JONATHAN MACY, author of *In the Shadow of His Wings* and minister
> in the Church of England

"Angels are everywhere! Until I read this book, I must confess that even as a Bible teacher I'd missed how *ever present* angels are at key junctures and in critical ways *throughout* the biblical story. As a pastor, I'd been mostly blind to the angels all around us (which most people in our church body, statistics show, more readily see). This wonderful book opened not only my eyes but my ears to the beautiful hum of angels surrounding us—a harmony that points us to the melody of Jesus at the center."

> —JOSHUA RYAN BUTLER, pastor at Imago Dei Community, Portland,
> OR; author of *The Skeletons in God's Closet* and *The Pursuing God*

"I make a practice of reading everything Scot McKnight writes because I learn so much from his bright mind and generous spirit. His work exemplifies an intelligent, rich way of understanding the Bible; and this wonderful book is no exception. After having read *The Hum of Angels,* I'll walk through my day with more awareness of God's loving presence and comfort, and more hope because of it."

> —SHAUNA NIEQUIST, *New York Times* best-selling author of *Present*
> *over Perfect*

"In *The Hum of Angels,* Scot McKnight invites us to consider the active and significant role angels play on the pages of Scripture and in fulfilling the purposes of God today—not for the sake of information, but for the sake of hope. How easy it is for us, from our ground-level perspective, to give discouragement and despair the upper hand. This reminder of the powerful activity of myriads of God's angels on our behalf is one more reason for hope to thrive in the future of God's ultimate victory over evil. This book is an eye-opening, reassuring, and hope-filled read."

—CAROLYN CUSTIS JAMES, author of *Half the Church: Recapturing God's Global Vision for Women* and *Malestrom: Manhood Swept into the Currents of a Changing World*

THE
HUM OF
ANGELS

Books by Scot McKnight

The Heaven Promise: Engaging the Bible's Truths About Life to Come

The Jesus Creed: Loving God, Loving Others

Embracing Grace: Discovering the Gospel that Restores Us to God, Creation, and Ourselves

Praying with the Church: Following Jesus Daily, Hourly, Today

The Blue Parakeet: Rethinking How You Read the Bible

Fasting

One Life: Jesus Calls, We Follow

The King Jesus Gospel: The Original Good News Revisited

Kingdom Conspiracy: Returning to the Radical Mission of the Local Church

A Fellowship of Differents: Showing the World God's Design for Life Together

THE HUM OF ANGELS

SCOT McKNIGHT

WATERBROOK

THE HUM OF ANGELS

All Scripture quotations, unless otherwise indicated, are taken from the Holy Bible, New International Version®, NIV®. Copyright © 1973, 1978, 1984, 2011 by Biblica Inc.® Used by permission. All rights reserved worldwide. Scripture quotations marked (KJV) are taken from the King James Version. Scripture quotations marked (NRSV) are taken from the New Revised Standard Version Bible, copyright © 1989, Division of Christian Education of the National Council of the Churches of Christ in the USA. Used by permission. All rights reserved.

Italics in Scripture quotations reflect the author's added emphasis.

Details in some anecdotes and stories have been changed to protect the identities of the persons involved.

Hardcover ISBN 978-1-60142-631-4
eBook ISBN 978-1-60142-633-8

Copyright © 2017 by Scot McKnight

Cover design by Kristopher K. Orr

Published in the United States by WaterBrook, an imprint of the Crown Publishing Group, a division of Penguin Random House LLC, New York.

WATERBROOK® and its deer colophon are registered trademarks of Penguin Random House LLC.

Library of Congress Cataloging-in-Publication Data
    Names: McKnight, Scot, author.
    Title: The hum of angels : listening for the messengers of God around us / Scot Mcknight.
    Description: First Edition. | Colorado Springs, Colorado : WaterBrook, 2017. Includes bibliographical references.
    Identifiers: LCCN 2016040290 (print) | LCCN 2016049191 (ebook) | ISBN 9781601426314 (hardcover) | ISBN 9781601426338 (electronic)
    Subjects: LCSH: Angels.
    Classification: LCC BT966.3 .M36 2017 (print) | LCC BT966.3 (ebook) | DDC 235/.3—dc23
    LC record available at https://lccn.loc.gov/2016040290

Printed in the United States of America
2017—First Edition

10 9 8 7 6 5 4 3 2 1

SPECIAL SALES
Most WaterBrook books are available at special quantity discounts when purchased in bulk by corporations, organizations, and special-interest groups. Custom imprinting or excerpting can also be done to fit special needs. For information, please e-mail specialmarketscms@penguinrandomhouse.com or call 1-800-603-7051.

For Gil and Lesley Smith

Therefore we praise you, joining our voices with
Angels and Archangels and with all the company of
heaven, who for ever sing this hymn to proclaim the
glory of your Name:

Holy, Holy, Holy Lord, God of power and might,
heaven and earth are full of your glory.
Hosanna in the highest.
Blessed is he who comes in the name of the Lord.
Hosanna in the highest.
—THE BOOK OF COMMON PRAYER,
PREFACE AND THE SANCTUS

CONTENTS

PART 4: GOD'S LOVING TRANSFORMATION
THROUGH ANGELS

Part 1

In Defense of Angels

THE HUM OF ANGELS

I was visiting a bird-supplies store when I mentioned to the owner that my wife and I had owned a hummingbird feeder but had never once seen a hummer at the feeder, so we tossed it out. I concluded that there were no hummers near our home.

The shop owner asked where we lived, I told him, and then he said, "They are there. Not only do some of your neighbors have hummers on their feeders, but hummers are all over the village." What he said next was the take-home line: "You just have to have eyes to see them. Once you do, you will see them everywhere. They are small and fast and camouflaged, but they are not that hard to spot."

Eventually we bought a new feeder, filled it, and waited until our eyes got accustomed to the sight of hummers. Kris and I now see them everywhere. When other people go on a walk with us, we often observe a hummer—but it is rare that our friends spot one. It takes experience. You need to learn to spot them out of the side of your eyes and acclimate to their habits of zooming and darting and taking shelter on obscure branches and even on telephone lines. But once you've learned to spot a hummer you will see them everywhere because they are everywhere.

Like angels. They, too, are all around us. Few of us have seen one because we first have to learn what we are looking for. In a good book about angels, Martin Israel, quoting a friend, wrote this: "Eternity lies all round us and only a veil prevents us seeing it."[1] The hum of angels surrounds us, and we only need ears to hear it or eyes to see them. Or perhaps a special sense for them. After all, the Bible tells us that Balaam's donkey could see an angel that Balaam himself could not see. The passage suggests that Balaam was so insensitive to God that he failed to notice.* At the end of her survey of angels, Jane Williams, author of an important book on angels, invites us to hear and join in the chorus:

> Behind, around, underneath, and through the day-to-day world that we inhabit is the song of the angels. It is beautiful, endless, joyful, and terrible. It will be sung whether we join in with it or not, but imagine the sensation of stepping into that angelic harmony and being caught up in its power and majesty. This is what the angels invite us to do. They long to teach us their song, so that we, with them, can sing a hymn of praise to the glorious universe and its maker.[2]

It should not bother us that dimensions of reality exist that we cannot see. Dogs can hear sounds we cannot hear; birds can migrate up and down the globe with a sense of direction that far exceeds our own; those little hummingbirds somehow know when to head north and when to head south, and all of a sudden they disappear from our summer feeders. Their sense of timing is unerring. Squirrels can somehow smell or feel nuts planted underground for winter storage; and bees . . . well, bees are a world unto themselves.

And those examples are just a few of the creatures living on earth. God knows vastly more than we do; God sees and senses vastly deeper than do we. So why should we think that only what we see, hear, or sense is all there is? There is a popular conviction that we can believe only in what we see and feel. The best word for this posture is *arrogance*. Bold and not beautiful.

Kris was driving through a wooded area the other day on the way to her office when a deer, seeming to suddenly notice her, stopped just before running into her lane of traffic. Had it continued on its initial path, Kris could have been in a serious accident. The timing was right for it to have happened. But she called me later and said the deer's moves were so unusual she wondered if she had been protected by an angel.

As it is with spotting hummingbirds, experience is our teacher. Kris's story re-

---

* Numbers 22:21–31

minds me of another one. At the time of this previous experience, we did not consider the involvement of an angel. But on further reflection perhaps we should have. (Jet lag might have prevented us from thinking this way at the time.)

We were on vacation in Italy. After landing in Milan in the north, we drove east toward Venice and had as our first night a stop in Verona. Having arrived in Verona, we quickly realized the city seemed like circles inside circles. We asked someone for help, and he pointed us forward, but after just one curve we were lost again. And jet-lagged.

Suddenly a kind man appeared at our car window. I showed him the name of our hotel, and he said, "Can I get in your car? I'll direct you to the hotel." Which he did, and we were overjoyed. We got out of our car and turned to thank him, but he seemed to disappear with a shuffle of his feet and a walk down the street. Was that man the hum of an angel? Perhaps so. Angels are everywhere, but you have to have an ear tuned to their hum, an ear sensitive enough to be surprised by angels.

Here are a few more things we learned from the gentleman at the bird-supplies store, who is a walking hummingbird encyclopedia. These brilliantly designed birds can fly in all directions and they consume thirty times their weight each day. They get into aerial combat with one another over who controls which feeders in the neighborhood. The man at the shop has studied data accumulated over centuries, and he speaks authoritatively and accurately.

The same can be said about those who seek to accumulate knowledge about angels. One angel passage in the Bible will give us something, a bit like Kris's and my limited experience with ruby-throated hummingbirds at our backyard feeder. (We've never seen any other kind of hummer there, but dozens of kinds of hummers populate the world.) The same is true with learning about angels. But if we look carefully at all the passages in the Bible that speak of or about angels and then read up on what theologians and historians have said, we can know plenty about them.

BELIEF IN GOD, BELIEF IN ANGELS

The hum of angels has been heard by theologians and pastors and priests, to be sure, but far more often by ordinary lay folks. Angels have been spotted by men and women and old folks and young adults. Doctors and lawyers and scientists and mechanics and landscapers and truck drivers all have seen them. Angels are no respecter of persons in their disclosures. Some people experience angels at a birth, others around the time of a loved one's death. Sometimes angels are seen by a dying person and other times by loved ones who attend to the dying. Sometimes people experience an angel at the moment their loved one dies a great distance away. Bible readers know that some angels appear during a person's sleep—and this, too, is common today.

Most people who experience angels don't tell anyone, or if they do, they tell only a person or two. And in light of the skepticism of our scientific world, those who spot angels often make it clear they are not "that kind of person." But even so they do think they saw an angel. The irony of our scientific age is that many people claim to have been visited by an angel in a hospital, and often enough it is a physician or nurse who reports the event.[3]

The most scientifically trained people in our world encounter angels. And speaking of scientists, no one is more scientific than astronauts who occupy a world of cold, mathematical calculations. They reside at the edge of harnessing immense energies, and some of them claim to have seen angels in space.[4] But many other people in this scientific age are afraid to talk about their experiences, thinking they won't be believed. One man has seen angels hovering every Sunday during services at his church, but when he told his priest about it, the priest ridiculed him.[5] Some believe, some don't. Back and forth the conversation goes.

Belief in God slides across the spectrum from "Lots of people believe in God" to "Fine, but keep it to yourself" and on to "The world is made up of different sorts, even believers." It slides from the acceptance of God as a normal belief to being considered (barely) tolerable. And belief in angels is met with even greater cynicism. Typically, the person who has experienced an angel is met with the hardly gentle question, "Are you serious?" That silences many who have angel stories to tell.

Andy Angel, a professor of New Testament and an expert on angels in the biblical world, sums up the situation well:

The embarrassing question is, of course, *are angels real?* Belief in God is generally socially acceptable. Even people who view religious faith as something of a vice tend to acknowledge that intelligent people can (for whatever reason!) believe in God. However, this grace does not extend as far as angels. Even among religious people there can be something of an embarrassment surrounding the subject of angels.[6]

While these might appear to be two very different issues, the question about angels is closely tied to the question about an "invisible" God. Allow me to append a defense to Angel's statement. The question is not first "Do you believe in angels?" but "Do you believe in God?" If you answer, "Yes, I believe in an invisible (and bodiless) God," you have all but said, "Yes, I can believe in invisible (and bodiless) angels too." Or you think invisible beings exist, which surely makes belief in angels at least reasonable. Something, or better yet Someone, doesn't have to be or have a body to exist.

Andy Angel has spelled this out in some intellectual categories. "If God exists, then bodiless Mind does exist. The existence of incorporeal spirit is no longer impossible. Belief in the existence of an incorporeal spirit is no longer irrational. Thus belief in angels is no longer irrational."[7] If God, who cannot be seen, exists, why would anyone refuse to believe in lesser-but-just-as-invisible angels and spirits? If we grant the reality of an invisible world, the supernatural, a reality just beyond ours, why would we put limits on what's out there?

Here is my claim: "If you believe in God, you also believe in angels." This is not a philosophical book about angels, nor is it an attempt to prove the reality of angels. I'm thankful the philosophers and apologists have set forth persuasive arguments in favor of angels and so have cleared the way for me to talk about what the Bible says about angels. I will do just that on the basis that belief in angels is intellectually credible.[8] Instead of my attempting to prove the reality of angels, I invite you to dig in with me to see what the Bible says about angels.[9] Here is a foretaste: there are far more angels-related passages in the Bible than most Christians know. The Bible, we will see, describes this world as full of wondrous beings, many beyond the scope of our eyes.

We can embrace the view that this empirical world is not all that exists. We can assert that there is an enchanted world where the natural and the supernatural overlap. If you accept this, know that some of the world's finest minds are on your side when it comes to believing in angels.

But there also are plenty of critics.

But for Centuries People Haven't Heard the Hum of Angels?

Old Testament professor Claus Westermann made this claim as he dismissed belief in angels:[10] "People don't believe in angels anymore. They haven't believed in angels for centuries." Westermann went on to say that, even though there is no such being as an angel, many of us still talk as though they exist. He offered this explanation: what the Bible calls an angel was not a supernatural being but rather a moment so important to someone that the person depicted it as an encounter with a messenger of God.

> The stories in the Bible that speak of angels relate the experiences of men and women to whom God drew so very near in moments of great personal crisis or danger that they sensed in the words of a human being the work of a messenger of God, and in the help of a human hand they felt the helping hand of God.[11]

Professors are not alone in doubting the reality of angels. A life of service in the church, including sermons, seminary education, and even church discussions, led Charles Jaekle to acknowledge that the church itself has ignored angels. Here is how he put it: "Reflection on a lifetime of church membership leads to one conclusion: *a massive bias that angels and their encounters with human beings are unworthy of serious religious study or investigation.*"[12]

If angels are absent from sermons and seminary education, a message is being sent loud and indirect: angels are not for public discussion. We could call this the "de-angelification" of the Bible, the church, and the faith. One result is that the many who have experienced angels have to be submerged in the "spiritual underground." They don't want to be considered cranks. Hence, for someone such as

Westermann, the so-called angels of the Bible were not angels but moments when a human said something so important that the breakthrough was explained *as if it were a messenger from God.* Westermann is far from alone in making such a claim.

Skepticism regarding the Bible's supernatural elements might well be a reaction to extravagant claims that have been made about the supernatural. To be sure, the medievals did love their angels and "knew" or sought to know all sorts of things about them. One of the world's great experts on angels in history, Valery Rees, points to the extravagances:

> [The famous theologian Thomas] Aquinas asked whether angels could see God, how they knew what they knew, whether they had knowledge of particular things, how they moved, and whether time affects them. People wanted to know how many angels there are, and exactly when they were created—or if they are still being created.[13]

Inquiring minds want to know, the saying goes. Excesses require strong reactions at times. And when it comes to angels, many reactions are just as excessive in the other direction. Yes, there have been angel extravagances aplenty. Still, surprising numbers of people continue to believe in old-fashioned, supernatural angels who appear and suddenly disappear. Rare would be the hospital or hospice pastor who does not have at least one story about angels. So Westermann was just wrong when he wrote, "People don't believe in angels anymore." They do and we do, or at least most of us do. One can't dismiss angels with a simple shrug of the shoulders.[14] Shrugging one's shoulders about angels, in fact, just might stir one of them up!

2

MOST OF US BELIEVE IN ANGELS

God and angels belong together, but still we must choose to believe in angels just as we must choose to believe in God. Jane Williams, a well-known British theologian and wife of Rowan Williams, former archbishop of Canterbury, has expressed this choice elegantly. "We can either live in our own small world, where we need serve nobody but ourselves, or we can live in a world of angels, people, principalities, and powers, which will commit us to action in helping to shape what kind of a world this will be."[1]

On Jane's side is this: *most* of us have chosen to believe in God and angels. The Bible talks frequently about angels, and Jewish literature beyond the Bible talks about angels just as much. The early Christians—and this is not too strong a statement—all believed in angels. Across the spectrum of religions, there is a widespread belief in angels. On matters in which philosophies and religions agree, one ought at least pause to consider why it is that humans always have believed in angels and spirits, both good and bad. Two historians of angels, Peter Marshall and Alexandra Walsham, stand with the consensus of humanity: "Seen and unseen, in heaven and on the earth, in image and in text, angels have persistently infiltrated the cultural imagination of western and near-eastern civilisation for more than two millennia." And on the next page they take us from the *always* to the *recent:* "The early modern world simply abounded with angels."[2] The present modern world and the postmodern world also abound in angels.

"Most of Us"

It needs to be emphasized that "most of us" believe in angels. The Baylor Religion Survey, one of the most highly respected surveys of what Americans believe, asked respondents if they believe in angels. The results show that

- 88 percent of women and 74 percent of men believe in angels,
- overall, 82 percent of Americans believe in angels,
- and 93 percent of the "religious" believe, but only 69 percent of the "spiritual" do.

The survey was conducted between 2005 and 2007, and it shows that more than eight in ten Americans believe angels exist.[3] That is far and away most of us. Further, a report that one-third of us claim to have seen an angel spurred well-known religious-experience researcher and reporter Emma Heathcote-James into action.[4] Perhaps the shrug of the shoulders about angels noted earlier ought to be directed at those who choose *not* to believe.

In December 2011, amid growing reports of the decline of religion, the Associated Press-GfK asked churchgoers about their belief in angels and found that

- 88 percent of Christians believe in angels,
- 95 percent of evangelical Christians believe,
- 94 percent of those who attend any kind of religious institution believe,
- and 77 percent of American adults overall believe in angels.[5]

Again, based on the Associated Press-GfK, most of us believe in angels. I give an example from a newspaper. Major-league baseball player Nick Swisher believes in angels; he has an angel tattoo under his shirt. It reminds him of a very private but important story.

As told by Anthony McCarron,

The tattoo sits on his chest, right near Nick Swisher's heart: "BLS," his grandmother's initials, with angel's wings and a halo. It is a remarkable tribute to Betty Lorraine Swisher, the woman Swisher calls the love of his life and an inspiration. . . .

Swisher's parents—his father, Steve, is a former major-league catcher—
divorced when he [Swisher] was in eighth grade and he moved into his
grandparents' house in Parkersburg, West Virginia. His grandmother kept
the loquacious Swisher in line. . . . "She turned me into a man, she really did,
and I can't thank her enough for it."

Betty Swisher died of brain cancer on Aug. 14, 2005. [Swisher's grand-
father, Donald, also has passed away.] Both are a part of his daily life, though,
in part through a series of baseball rituals that any Yankee fan has probably
noticed.

He has both of their initials scrawled on the bottom of the handle of all
his bats and he usually kisses that spot before he goes to the plate. Then he
looks upward to recognize them again.[6]

During the Kansas City Royals' post-World Series celebrations in 2015, fans
heard more about angels in America's game:[7] "I think we had some angels on our
side," said Royals third baseman Mike Moustakas, one of three Royals players who
lost a parent not long before the series began, suggested that in this series they had
angels looking out for them. Big, brawny athletes who have been deeply moved by
the death of parents think of their departed parents as angels, which at least suggests
they really do believe in angels.

In this book we want to ask about what the Bible says about angels and what it
says to very common beliefs, including the belief that we become angels at death.
Does the Bible teach that humans become angels in eternity? Where do we get the
idea that our favorite people—saints or otherwise—become angels when they die?
I've heard more than one person say, most often about the tragic death of children,
"They are angels now." I just saw a tweet that read, "My angel died three months
ago." It is striking how often the word *angel* gets attached to those we love. Why call
loved ones angels? We need to see what the Bible says about common beliefs such as
this. What the Bible shares with most of us is a belief in angels.

Leaders in the church measure theology by the great theologians. So I grab the
list of "great" theologians in Gerald McDermott's *The Great Theologians: A Brief*

Guide.[8] Here they are: Origen, Athanasius, Augustine, Thomas Aquinas, Martin Luther, John Calvin, Jonathan Edwards, Friedrich Schleiermacher, John Henry Newman, Karl Barth, and Hans Urs von Balthasar. Apart from Schleiermacher, who predictably set angels aside in his creation of modern Protestant liberalism, *every one* of the other great theologians believed in angels. These are nothing but the greatest minds in the history of the church. I'm not afraid to say it: not only do "most of us" believe in angels, the "best of us" when it comes to theology also believe in angels.

The most influential theologian of the twentieth century, the Swiss theologian Karl Barth, threw down the gauntlet. In his famous multivolume study of what Christians believe, called *Church Dogmatics,* Barth essentially said, *Take God and the angels or drop both, but God without the angels is impossible.*

According to Barth:

> It is true, of course, that we can miss the angels. We can deny them altogether. We can dismiss them as superfluous, or absurd and comic. . . . *If we cannot or will not accept angels, how can we accept what is told us by the history of Scripture, or the history of the Church, or the history of the Jews, or our own life's history? . . . Where God is, there the angels of God are. Where there are no angels, there is no God.*[9]

It may seem to be the sophisticated thing to classify belief in angels with belief in myths and superstitions and fairies and hobbits. It may be considered a mark of intelligence to lower one's head and peer over one's trendy glasses at the believer in angels with a look of condescension. But on this one the so-called sophisticates are not trending. Karl Barth here expresses the foundation of *The Hum of Angels:* The Bible is God's Word, the Bible teaches about angels, and God and angels are tied together in the Christian faith. Read again what he wrote: "Where there are no angels, there is no God." That from the twentieth century's most influential theologian.

Most of us believe in angels. But what are we to do with the extravagances and all the angel encounters we read about? That is a fair question.

THE YES AND NO ABOUT ANGELS

When there is too much emphasis on angels, some of us plead for sanity and, hence, less emphasis on angels. And when the supernatural world begins to be pushed aside, as took place after the Enlightenment, others begin to urge listeners to accept the reality of angels. Protestants always have been divided over how to view stories of people who experienced angels, but they are devoted to believing in angels when it comes to teaching the Bible. Here's an older but apt illustration of this.

Raymond Gillespie, a professor of history at the National University of Ireland, Maynooth, and an expert on angels, sketched how angels have been approached in Ireland, a land deeply divided between Protestants (mostly in Northern Ireland) and Roman Catholics in the Republic of Ireland. He found a debate between two Protestant ministers in a record of Irish church history. Henry Piers and James Leigh differed over the issue of angels in Irish worship, prayers, and spirituality. (This sounds like a joke is coming, but it is not.) Leigh pressed Piers on the presence of angels in the regular prayer recited from the prayer book, which states "the intercession of saints *and angels* for us." Their debate raised the issue of who was the more Protestant (or faithful). Gillespie summed up their debate with what might be called the Protestant dilemma regarding angels:

> They could not abandon the notion [of the reality of angels], since it was
> biblical and provided a language with which to describe events that were
> otherwise mysterious. Neither could they embrace traditional angelology,
> since that elaborate discourse was tinged with Catholic scholasticism.[10]

For these old-timers, the worry was if they got too biblical they might get too Catholic. And if they went too far the other way and denied angels, they would no longer be Protestant or biblical.

It is undeniable. Most of us believe in angels. But why?

THREE REASONS WHY SO MANY
OF US BELIEVE IN ANGELS

Ten years ago professor Michael Rogness discovered five shelves of books about angels in a bookstore. That accounts for one hundred twenty-one separate titles on angels![1] Author and former pastor Eugene Peterson once explained the presence of angels in the novels of John Irving (*A Prayer for Owen Meany*), Robertson Davies (*What's Bred in the Bone*), C. S. Lewis (*Out of the Silent Planet, Perelandra, That Hideous Strength*), and Reynolds Price (*The Tongues of Angels*). Peterson referred to the appearance of angels in these works as witnesses to transcendence.[2] You need not look long to find angels in literature.

THREE REASONS FOR BELIEVING

Why do people believe in angels and a transcendent cosmic order? My studies reveal three basic reasons.

The Bible
The Bible includes some three hundred references or allusions to angels. Angels appear most often when God is about to alter the course of history, but they exist in the background all the time. In fact, Martin Israel, after a splendid romp through the angel passages of the Old Testament, concluded that the Bible is a "hive of angelic activity."[3]

The vast host of angels carries out a vast host of tasks in the Bible. They disclose information and good news and comfort; guide and protect and fight; worship and lead in worship. In all this, one thing is clear: they are all over the Bible. They are in the Garden of Eden (or at the gate); they visit Abraham and Moses and the prophets. In one episode after another, they are present with Jesus, from the cradle to the cross to the empty tomb to the Ascension. And they make their usual visitations to the apostles Paul, Peter, and John.

Many think the opening line of the Bible—"In the beginning God created the *heavens* and the earth"—acknowledges the reality of the heavenly realm filled with angels and supernatural beings. The big-ticket item here is the Nicene Creed, which affirms this interpretation. It holds that God made all things "visible and invisible." To create the "heavens," then, means for careful students of the creed that God created heaven as an invisible space for invisible angels and spirits. God, who is invisible to us but all knowing and all encompassing, dwells in that space called heaven.

Author Martin Israel, who lectures medical doctors, has concluded "that we are encompassed in a blanket of angelic activity. In the course of daily life, we (apart from a few profoundly mystical people) are closed to the presence of angels (except perhaps in a great crisis), for we tend to be very easily distracted by worldly matters." Israel is describing a common modern condition here, but he shows that it still is possible to hear the hum of angels. "An open heart and a generous attitude to life are features that make us especially amenable to angelic communication, the closed mind and stony heart resist the ingress of angelic activity."[4]

Author and sage Frederick Buechner has an open heart and ears, so he hears the hum more than most of us.

> Sleight-of-hand magic is based on the demonstrable fact that as a rule people
> see only what they expect to see. Angels are powerful spirits whom God sends
> into the world to wish us well. Since we don't expect to see them, we don't.
> An angel spreads its glittering wings over us, and we say things like, "It was
> one of those days that made you feel good just to be alive," or "I had a hunch
> everything was going to turn out all right" or "I don't know where I ever
> found the courage."[5]

Many have closed their ears to the hum of angels, but others have chosen to listen to the Bible and so believe in angels. (I'm with them.) Again, there are some three hundred references to angels in the Bible, and we might return to the end of chapter 2 to remind ourselves what Karl Barth asked: "If we cannot or will not accept angels, how can we accept what is told us by the history of Scripture, or the history of the Church, or the history of the Jews, or our own life's history?"[6]

Some of the brightest theological lights of our day have also observed that angels are sent on mission to speak the message of God to humans. Angels are, then, like the Bible in being God's communication with us. Likewise, the Bible is like the angels in God's communication with us. The Bible leads some to believe in angels, and angels help us read the Bible in a way that is open to God's transcendent communication.

Experiences

Some people believe in angels because they've seen an angel. Like Peter Martin. During Advent in Martin's tony church, Saint Thomas Episcopal Church on Fifth Avenue in Manhattan, the leaders were singing carols and reading lessons and processing past the pulpit when Peter saw the angel. Here's how he has described it:

> It expanded my mind, because it looked like super HD. The colors and
> reality of it were illuminated and exceptional like the reality of Heaven in
> C. S. Lewis's *The Great Divorce*. . . . It had huge wings and held a huge
> sword and wore a suit of armor, and the colors were just dazzling: golds and
> blues and reds. It sort of looked like fine needlepoint, but of course it wasn't.
> But it was incredible. It was just sort of looking over the whole congregation.[7]

Martin said he was "utterly thrilled and just completely bathed in its fearsome and awesome beauty." When it comes to churches, you will find none that are more trendy, Western, or sophisticated than a Manhattan Episcopal church. But it was there that, during the singing of a Christmas carol, Peter Martin encountered an angel.

Tara Beth Leach, my former assistant at Northern Seminary in Lombard,

Illinois, and now the senior pastor at The First Church of the Nazarene of Pasadena, California, told me of her own angel experience. When she was a college student, she felt called to teach and preach. But such a calling tore at her heart because she knew some in the church didn't think preaching was what God called women to do. While journaling with tears in her eyes and in deep prayer in her dorm room, she saw a bright light on a wall. She then turned to see a light in the corner of the room. She heard an "inaudible" voice that told her it was all right, God was guiding, and God was with her. As she worked with me on researching angels, that long-forgotten experience came back to her. While she knows some claims of angel experiences are over the top, this study and her experience came together in a moment of confession that she, too, believes in angels.

Emma Heathcote-James, a chronicler of angel-encounter stories, has one to tell about herself. She and a friend climbed Mount Sinai one night. They wandered off to take pictures and lost track of time. As they headed back, they became disoriented on a precarious downhill hike. No one else was on the trail. They prayed, and Emma cried aloud. Here is how she describes what happened next.

> Firstly we kept seeing a person dressed in a long white garment on ledges
> below us. At the time, I believed it to be our group leader who, like most
> Arabs, was in fact wearing a white robe. But each time we reached the point
> where we had seen him, there was nothing there. This happened several
> times. Then, literally out of nowhere, a beautiful young couple appeared
> behind a big rock. It struck me immediately how manicured and well dressed
> they were despite the fact that they must have been climbing for six hours or
> so. . . . Strangely, [the woman] spoke perfect English. . . . Helping us over the
> worst terrain, they accompanied us to the bottom where we found our group
> and our *very* distraught leader who thought he'd lost us! We turned to thank
> the couple but they were nowhere to be seen.[8]

In her book *Seeing Angels,* Heathcote-James documents a number of stories like her own. In fact, around you are many who have encountered angels but are not sure they want anyone to know. Over lunch at the office sometime, ask about angels. You might be surprised what you hear. Many people believe in angels because they've *seen* angels.

Christian art

Others believe in angels because they have absorbed angels depicted in Christian art. On a recent sabbatical, Kris and I spent a few weeks in one of our favorite places, Assisi, Italy, home of the great Saint Francis. Assisi, you might guess, is graced with wonderful churches, not least the gorgeous Basilica di San Francesco, which is filled with art and frescoes by Giotto di Bondone and Ciambue. (Let your tongue loose and give "di Bondone" your best effort.) Angels abound in Assisi, and Kris dubbed one common type "chubby cherubs." In addition, there were seraphs, often adorned in wispy tunics trimmed in gold, held aloft by fluttering wings, and sometimes be-capped with a divine glow. At times they were blowing horns as an act of praise. Assisi's seraphs were, according to this male observer, effeminate. Every time I saw one, I made a mental correction. The Bible's angels and the angels of Jewish litera-ture from the New Testament period (or before) are male figures. They are mighty warriors and intimidating presences. In fact, the term *seraph* derives from the He-brew word for fire (*sarap*). A bolt or flash or pillar of fire is a far distance from a wispy, ethereal, horn-blowing seraph seen in Christian art.

It is a little-known fact that the angels that appear in Jewish literature are some-times said to be circumcised. Not to put too fine a point on the observation, but one would have to ask who performed the act, and the answer is—*voila!*—they were created that way. That speaks to the maleness of angels and raises circumcision to the highest level. (But I digress.)

To take in Assisi's churches is to take the art of angels into one's heart. Giotto's angels have very human faces along with wings and halos, and they are never the center of the story: Jesus is. Some of Francis's followers thought he had himself be-come an angel after his death, which illustrates their admiration—but the little poor man called Francis needed some managers and filters, who should have kept the hagiography at a reasonable level. The official early biographer, Bonaventure, wrote that Francis "is seraphic; he is the angel of peace; and above all he is the sixth angel of the Apocalypse."[9] That's over the top. A few hundred years later another Franciscan, a specialist on angels, in nothing less than a flight into ethereal words, claimed Francis had been "alembicated into the human viscera."[10] (I had to look up *alembicated*: it means "overly refined." Viscera is the intestines. Now we're all stumped.) Whatever it means, I'm glad for Francis but am quite certain he's no angel. There is nothing in the Bible that indicates humans are transformed into angels upon death. In fact, the model for what we will be like after death is not angels but the resurrection body of Jesus—who, again, did not become an angel.

The numerous frescoes in the churches of Assisi help us understand why so many have accepted the reality of angels by absorbing Christian art. This art makes angels normal.

The chubby cherubs and wispy seraphs are like fingers pointing us somewhere, and if we follow the directions, those artistic representations will take us there. What these images do well is surround Jesus and acclaim Jesus and announce Jesus and draw our attention to Jesus. I sometimes wonder if Christians believe in angels from art because those images are so connected to Jesus, thus the adoration of Jesus is accompanied by belief in angels.

Peter Kreeft, whose skill in writing has made Aquinas's thick philosophical volume on angels accessible to one and all, reminds us of the importance of this art: it is symbolic and leads us to God.

> These images, from human artists' imaginations, are only symbolic. Wings symbolize speed, halos of light symbolize wisdom or heavenly holiness, harps symbolize the beauty of spiritual harmony, and cherubic babies symbolize innocence—all of which angels really possess.[11]

For a variety of reasons—among them the Bible, experiences people have, and art—the vast majority of Christians believe in angels. Belief in angels is a choice. We choose to believe that the world is more than what is tangible and this side of supernatural. It is a choice to believe in an invisible God accompanied by (mostly) invisible angels, and it is a choice to open one's heart to them.

Belief in angels is a starting point. Knowing what they are like helps complete the picture. Let's start with the four most important words about angels. Note that these words challenge the all-too-common ideas about angels as they also give us firmer footing for understanding what is happening in our world.

4

THE FOUR MOST IMPORTANT
WORDS ABOUT ANGELS

Believing in angels, as most of us do, is one thing. But how can we know what angels are really like?

Christians look to the Bible as the source of their faith. Or to use the words of theologians today, the Bible is the "norming norm" of what we are to think and believe and do. We know about angels on the basis of the Bible, and the Bible keeps us in check about what not to believe. In one of his many memorable statements, Karl Barth brought the Bible to our attention with these words: "The teacher and master to which we must keep in this matter [about angels] can only be the Holy Scriptures of the Old and New Testament, that we must not accept any other authority, that we must listen exhaustively to what this guide has to tell us, and that we must respect what it says and what it does not say."[1]

I stand with Barth: either we trust what God and the Spirit tell us in the Word about angels or we don't. Either we believe it because it is written, or we choose to believe what we choose to believe. While I do not discount the reality that angels still appear to humans, I stand with the Bible's understanding of angels. As a result, I will at times challenge accounts of modern encounters with angels that veer from the Bible's clear themes. So we will look closely at four biblical terms that clarify the deepest ideas about angels.

THEY ARE MESSENGERS FROM GOD

The Bible refers to angels more than two hundred times. The word *angel* comes from the Greek *angelos,* which means "messenger," a term used for, well, what we mean when we say "angel." The Hebrew word *malak* used in the Old Testament also means "messenger." The terms for angels can be used as much for a human as for a supernatural being. Angels are spirits, so they are called *angels* because they are spirit-messengers.

One biblical usage of *angel* perfectly illustrates the meaning of messenger. The apostle Paul said the Galatians received him as an "angel of God," that is, as a God-sent messenger.* They did not confuse him with a supernatural being, that's for sure! Angels are messengers, or *spirits on mission.*

This is stated clearly in the letter to the Hebrews.† Here is the verse in two translations, the New International Version and the New Revised Standard Version, and I have italicized the words that matter most:

> Are not all angels *ministering spirits sent to serve* those who will inherit salvation? (NIV)
>
> Are not all angels *spirits in the divine service, sent to serve* for the sake of those who are to inherit salvation? (NRSV)

The question is asked with the assumption that readers will respond: "Why yes, of course, we all know that." The original hearers were familiar enough with the Bible to know that angels are God's messengers sent on a mission.

We need a big cosmic sketch now, so bear with me because it will say something really important about angels. The Bible begins by telling us that God created *both* the heavens and the earth. Understanding earth as God's creation seems quite natural to us, but the heavens too are created and *so are the angels* who are in that heaven.

---

* Galatians 4:14
† Hebrews 1:14

Next item to add to the sketch: God for some reason chose to reside in heaven. We need to nuance this a bit. It is true that God is omnipresent, but it also is true that God resides in heaven in a special way. What makes heaven superior to earth is that God chose *to indwell heaven, to make decisions about earth from heaven, and to send* (here is where we have been headed) *his angels to earth from heaven.*

Final item in the sketch: the present heaven, where God dwells, combines God's *throne* room, God's *board* room, and God's *court* room. God rules, God contemplates, and God judges from heaven.

Now the angels come in. This same heaven is where the angels dwell. Just beyond mortal gaze, heaven is an alternate reality—created by God but not what we usually picture when we think of created reality. From that alternate created reality, God sends angels to earth to accomplish his purposes. Angels are heaven dwellers sent from heaven to earth for a specific mission.

As spirits sent on mission—as messengers—angels are limited to carrying out that mission. To be sure, they are supernatural beings. And yes, they dwell in the presence of God (lucky them!). But there are some things they cannot do.

> Angels cannot . . . save, redeem or liberate the earthly creature. They cannot
> forgive even the smallest sin, or remove even the slightest pain. They can do
> nothing to bring about the reconciliation of the world with God. Nor are
> they judges of the world. . . . They did not establish the covenant between
> God and man, and they cannot fulfill, maintain, renew or confirm it. They
> do not overcome death. They do not rule the history of salvation, or universal
> history, or any history.[2]

What they do is God's bidding. They are here, just beyond the eye's sight and ear's hearing. But with some sensitivity we can adjust our ears to the hum of angels. Wherever God is at work, his angels will be present as messengers sent for our redemption. Author Joel Miller has reminded us that "God sends his angels to live among us and lift our fallen humanity toward Christ."[3] Notice how clear their mission is in Miller's words: "to live among us and lift our fallen humanity toward Christ." He is a highly regarded editor and author, and if I were his editor I'd suggest changing his "and" to "to." They are among us *to* lift us to Christ!

How do angels do this messenger work? Once again, Miller helps us: they do their messenger work both invisibly and visibly. That is, they can communicate as God's messengers to us in our hearts, in our minds, in our souls, and in our spirits, *or* they can be messengers by assuming some type of visible form. It might be human or angelic form.[4] The primary mode of angelic communication described in the Bible is some kind of visible form.

We will return to this in later chapters. But for now, we will move to the second word that clarifies the work and identity of angels.

ANGELS ARE LEADERS IN REDEMPTIVE WORSHIP

What are angels doing in heaven with God? We need to look again at Hebrews 1:14 and take special notice of the term *ministering* (NIV) or even better, *divine service* (NRSV).

> Are not all angels *ministering* spirits sent to serve those who will inherit salvation?
>
> Are not all angels spirits *in the divine service,* sent to serve for the sake of those who are to inherit salvation?

The word behind these two English translations commonly refers to *serving in God's temple in a priestly manner.* The writer to the Hebrews knew his hearers were familiar with the work of priests in the temple. So angels are described as *commissioned by God to lead us earthbound humans into worship of God.* And if we push to the end of the verse, we see they are sent by God as part of our *redemption.* These worshiping spirits are sent by God to help in our redemption so we can join them in worshiping the God of redemption.

So the second most important description about angels is this: they *lead God's people in redemptive worship.* The last book of the Bible, the book of Revelation, makes this obvious. Angels in heaven are saturated with worship of God as a result of the Lamb's redemptive work. Notice (and please read) these beautiful verses of angel-led worship and intercession:*

> Then I looked and heard the voice of many angels, numbering thousands
> upon thousands, and ten thousand times ten thousand. They encircled the
> throne and the living creatures and the elders. In a loud voice they were saying:
>
> "Worthy is the Lamb, who was slain,
> to receive power and wealth and wisdom and strength
> and honor and glory and praise!" . . .
>
> All the angels were standing around the throne and around the elders
> and the four living creatures. They fell down on their faces before the throne
> and worshiped God, saying:
>
> "Amen!
> Praise and glory
> and wisdom and thanks and honor
> and power and strength
> be to our God for ever and ever.
> Amen!" . . .
>
> Another angel, who had a golden censer, came and stood at the altar. He
> was given much incense to offer, with the prayers of all God's people, on the
> golden altar in front of the throne. The smoke of the incense, together with
> the prayers of God's people, went up before God from the angel's hand.

---

* Revelation 5:11–12; 7:11–12; 8:3–4

This is a rich idea: angels are worship leaders. Images of angels can be spotted on some altars in the great cathedrals. In this art, angels are depicted offering incense, that is, the people's prayers. They are leaders in prayer, intercession, and worship.

Here then is my summary of our first two words: angels are *God-saturated and worshiping messengers* sent by God on mission with a message that can lead to our redemption. Angels are not the subject of the story. They are ministers in a story *about God*. Fascination with angel-messengers can inch dangerously close to idolatry.

The error of worshiping angels rather than God has emerged throughout history. In fact, the apostle Paul told the Colossian church not to worship angels. The apostle John had to be told not to worship an angel when one appeared to him.* Angels worship God and are sent on mission to lead us in that worship. Angels that don't summon us to see God[5] are not doing God's work. Rather, they are the rebellious, bad angels, often called "demons" or "evil spirits."

ANGELS ARE ACTIVE IN OUR WORLD

A third word will tie this all together. The word is *active*. Angels are not slouching toward earth on heavenly La-Z-Boy chairs. Rather, throughout the Bible and all through the Jewish literature written at the time of the New Testament, angels were actively involved—perhaps a bit snoopy at times—in all that was happening in heaven and earth. Andy Angel, after an informed sketch of Jewish literature about what angels were doing, summarized it in a long list of actions:[6]

So far from gazing wistfully into the middle distance, angels are anything but idle.

They *manage* the workings of the cosmos.

They *perform special tasks* at particular times, as required by the Almighty.

---

* Colossians 2:18; Revelation 22:8–9

They *intercede, pray for, and petition* the Lord on behalf of humanity (but the likelihood is that this role was taken over by Jesus, according to early Christians).

They *lead exemplary lives* in heaven, modeling holiness to humanity.

But pictures of angels with harps are not wholly wide of the mark. The chief role of angels is to worship God and in this they model the primary calling of all people. Indeed, their worship was understood to be so enthralling that some ancient Jews and Christians sought to join in the heavenly worship, but one of their number—the early Christ-follower, Paul—saw how the eagerness for experience was leading to arrogance rather than godliness. As a result, Paul urged his fellows to worship instead in humility and truth.

There is no improving this summary. (It is either found in or can be inferred from the Old Testament.) I would, however, draw our attention again to our theme: *angels are very, very busy beings.* One must imagine them constantly worshiping God and, out of that worship, being sent on missions to accomplish God's work on earth.

Angels are tasked to lead people to God. But there's something that draws me into wells of gratitude for the activities of angels. They are watching and curious about all that humans do because they *have divine concern for us.*

Angels Are Concerned About You and Me

I think my favorite set of lines in the Bible regarding angels is found in Peter's first letter, verses 10–12, and it moves from the prophets to the angels. Peter wrote about prophets and how their message kept a long eye on (and over) the horizon to see what God might be doing next. What the angels didn't know was that they were looking forward to Jesus as God's Messiah and true ruler of the empire. Here's how Peter expressed it:

It was revealed to them that they were not serving themselves but you, when
they spoke of the things that have now been told you by those who have
preached the gospel [about Jesus] to you by the Holy Spirit sent from heaven.*

Of all those mentioned in the Bible, surely the prophets are near the top for all
of us. They heard from God and in turn revealed to us what God wants us to know.
Though the Bible's narrative shows that God wanted to reveal his deepest message
over time, that narrative leads us to see that the deep message of God is about Jesus.
The angels seemed not to know elements of this deep message.

What Peter said about the prophets adds a special insight into angels. "Even
angels long to look into these things."† *Wow,* I say to myself. God's angels, those who
stand alongside God and worship God and lead the hosts of heaven in praise and
adoration, *are deeply curious about what God is doing in the world through Jesus.*
Angels are not like God in being omniscient. They are like us. They have vast pock-
ets of ignorance. And they are *curious beings.* Peter depicted angels as those who
have their hands on a window sill and pull themselves up high enough to peer into
the kitchen to see what Mom's baking for dinner, or as explorers who have come
upon a massive precipice and creep to the edge of the precipice so they can peer into
the deep chasm. Angels are curious like that.

Another verse in the Bible refers to angels as "watchers" or "a watchman." It is
found in Daniel 4:13:

In the visions I saw while lying in bed, I looked, and there before me was a
holy one, *a messenger* [NRSV: "a holy watcher"], coming down from heaven.

Such an idea about God having "watchers" who scan the cosmos and hear what
is being said and report back to God is found in a number of places in the Bible and
in related writings.‡

---

* 1 Peter 1:12
† 1 Peter 1:12.
‡ Notice what is said in context at Daniel 3:28; 8:16; 10:13. This theme is developed extensively of the fallen angels
  in the pseudepigraphal book 1 Enoch 1–36.

There is more. Paul wrote that angels are watching the course of history in a way that is similar to the way you and I may become engrossed in a movie, a news report, or a good book. "We have been made a spectacle to the whole universe," Paul wrote, "to angels as well as to human beings."* He exhorted women to dress as earthlings who are aware they are being watched by angels.† He later told his favorite young pastor, Timothy: "I charge you, in the sight of God and Christ Jesus *and the elect angels,* to keep these instructions."‡

In John Milton's beautiful and epic poem, *Paradise Lost,* angels are everywhere. They are talking and listening and watching and reporting and revealing. Is this what the Bible teaches about angels? A qualified "yes" but still, soundly "yes." Why are they depicted like this in Peter's letter and elsewhere? It is because angels *care.*

Angels care in this order: (1) they care about God's glory, (2) they care about God's Son, Jesus, and God's mission, and so (3) they care that humans enter into the life-giving, eternal mission of grace and redemption and joy. Angels care that we are full of joy and that we are happy. This is why they burst into song, praise, and jubilation when anyone turns to God in repentance and faith. Notice what Jesus said about the joy of angels:

> I tell you that in the same way there will be more *rejoicing in heaven* over one sinner who repents than over ninety-nine righteous persons who do not need to repent. . . .
>
> In the same way, I tell you, there is *rejoicing in the presence of the angels of God* over one sinner who repents.§

In the next paragraph in this chapter in Luke's Gospel, the father, who is like God, throws a colossal party for his lost and now found son. The revelers in that heavenly party are the angels. They exult with joyous carols, not because they are automated like some jukebox, but because they are curious and they care. They are filled with joy in God's own joy. The early Christian fathers depicted the ascension

---

* 1 Corinthians 4:9
† 1 Corinthians 11:10
‡ 1 Timothy 5:21
§ Luke 15:7, 10

of Jesus as something that caused amazement and wonder and praise among the angels. This can be true only because the angels care; they don't know what's happening next and so are utterly dumbfounded by the glories of what God did in Christ. Even the angels were kept in the dark about the sending of Christ to earth and his return to rule in glory![7] As we read what the Bible says about angels, we will need to look for their curiosity about what is to happen, their anticipation of God's redemptive work in Christ, and their profound exultation when Christ accomplishes his mission.

Before we summarize these four most important words about angels, we have one question to answer: What about the cherubs and the seraphs? Are they angels too?

ARE CHERUBS AND SERAPHS ANGELS?

Yes and no. In the beginning, we recall, God made the heavens and the earth. The earth is our home while heaven is the home for angels and for all supernatural beings invisible to you and to me. An angel is a spirit, or a supernatural being, sent on a mission as a messenger. The word *angel* is not the only term used for what we often call angels today. For instance, at the exit to the Garden of Eden, there were "cherubim and a flaming sword flashing back and forth to guard the way to the tree of life" and the Bible says in Psalms in another context that God "mounted the cherubim and flew."* So are the cherubs (in Hebrew the plural is *cherubim*) angels? What about the seraphim of Isaiah 6: "Then one of the seraphim flew to me with a live coal in his hand."† Are they angels? Some say yes; some say no.

It is clear from the Bible that cherubs and seraphs are *not* messengers in the strict sense that angels are. Yet it also can be said they are accomplishing a mission from God. This might seem confusing, but I believe there's a simple answer: *cherubs* and *seraphs* are but two kinds of spiritual beings created by God to inhabit the heavens. There are others, such as the "four living creatures" of Revelation 4:6–11, where we read:

---

* Genesis 3:24 and Psalm 18:10
† Isaiah 6:6

In the center, around the throne, were *four living creatures,* and they were covered with eyes, in front and in back. The *first living creature* was like a lion, the *second* was like an ox, the *third* had a face like a man, the *fourth* was like a flying eagle. *Each of the four living creatures* had six wings and was covered with eyes all around, even under its wings. Day and night they never stop saying:

> " 'Holy, holy, holy
> is the Lord God Almighty,'
> who was, and is, and is to come."

Whenever *the living creatures* give glory, honor and thanks to him who sits on the throne and who lives for ever and ever, the twenty-four elders fall down before him who sits on the throne and worship him who lives for ever and ever. They lay their crowns before the throne and say:

> "You are worthy, our Lord and God,
>   to receive glory and honor and power,
> for you created all things,
>   and by your will they were created
>   and have their being."

These four living creatures sound a bit like the cherubs of the Old Testament, and they have wings like the seraphs of Isaiah 6. But in this passage from Revelation, they are described in terms that do not echo the appearance of either cherubs or seraphs. And they are not called angels either. So what are they? They are *other supernatural beings* that inhabit God's created heaven. If we use the term *angels*—as I prefer to do—for supernatural beings that dwell in heaven with God, then it is fine to call cherubs and seraphs angels. Either way, biblical references to cherubs and seraphs add to the population and praise of God in God's presence.

SUMMARY

The four most important terms about angels lead us to this: angels are but one type of heavenly being that are *God-saturated* and *worshiping* beings. Because angels are so active and concerned about the earth, God sends them to accomplish redemption. I am not opposed to angel experiences today; I have family and friends who have experienced angels. But the Bible makes clear that angels don't appear to us for the thrill of the moment or to prove we are spiritual or to supply evidence of an alternative reality. Angels dwell in the presence of God, and they appear to us *only if and when* God sends them on mission for our redemption.

To deepen that sense of redemptive mission on the part of angels, I want now to explore their various missions. We begin on a note of grace: underneath the angels, behind the angels, to the side of the angels, and above the angels is our glorious God of love. Every mission that angels serve on earth is an expression of God's love for us.

Part 2

GOD'S LOVING PRESENCE IN ANGELS

ANGELS EXPRESS GOD'S LOVE

Jonathan Macy, a scholar and pastor, is one of the world's experts on angels. He has pointed a long finger at too much speculation regarding angels and instead points us toward the pastoral ministry of angels.

> Do any angels in Scripture appear and then, before anything else, say something like: "Behold, I am an immaterial heavenly being of awesome power and mysterious nature, who lives halfway up a celestial hierarchy. My supernatural knowledge has given me insight into your situation." No, they say, for example, "I am Gabriel," or "I am a fellow servant, with you and your brethren, who hold to the testimony of Jesus" (Luke 1:19; Revelation 19:10). More often than not they say *"Do not fear!"* to put people at their ease. These are descriptions based in relationship and service and a wish to communicate, not theological or philosophical categories. Angels have names. Angels converse with people. Angels are relational beings who, under God, serve God's people.[1]

Angels appear and immediately assure us not to be afraid because, though they are fierce and powerful beings, they are on our side. They are here for us, and they have a message for us from God. Angels, Macy wants us to see, do not appear to spur more speculation. They serve us for the joy of redemption. They are serious about our growth in grace; they are concerned that we fall in love with the glory of God and that we learn to worship God; and they long for our redemption. Macy has led me to realize that *any approach to angels that is not pastorally shaped fails to understand that the Bible describes angels as pastors.* They are sent to pastor us into the grace of God.

While I have learned much from Macy, I want to press behind his understanding of the pastoral ministry of angels. I want to look more closely at God's pastoral *love* expressed in angels. God sends angels to pastor us because God loves us. Angels, then, are expressions of nothing less than the love of God. In my previous writings, I have expressed an understanding of God's love that will guide us through the rest of this book Four themes of love will help us understand the pastoral mission of angels. (There is, after all, nothing like having a pastor sent straight from the throne room of God!)

GOD'S LOVE IN AN ANGEL

Tara Beth Leach, my former graduate assistant, received this story from someone she knows. It illustrates quite well that God loves us and occasionally sends angels our way to express that love.

> It was over sixteen years ago now, I was praying to the Lord early one morning and just asking for a sense of confirmation of His hand upon my life (as I would begin training to be a Salvation Army officer in a few months' time). I then headed off for work, and it was around 6:30 a.m. as I parked my car to walk to the train station. At that time of morning, there were never many people around, but as I got out of the car, there was an elderly gentlemen walking toward me . . . Something made me just say "this is an angel." The man came up to me and talked to me as I walked to the station and even told me that I worked in a bank, which was true. As we got near the entrance to the train station, he wished me well for the day, and as I turned round to say good-bye, he was suddenly gone. . . . Whether others would agree it was an angel, I don't know, but for me it was, and a sign of blessing, of God's

confirmation of His "walking with me" in my life's journey. . . . That
encounter [has] encouraged me countless times.

We will see other such stories in some of the chapters that follow, but this story
combines two features of what the Bible tells us about angels. First, they come from
a God who loves us, and second, we experience the angelic visitor as confirmation of
that love.

But what is love?

The word *love* often conveys only a small fraction of its meaning. A dozen years ago
I wrote a book on the importance of love in the spiritual vision of Jesus (*The Jesus
Creed: Loving God, Loving Others*). I could not come to terms with a definition that
made sense. One element that I was settled on was that the English dictionaries were,
well, not biblical. Which makes sense because English dictionaries inform us of what
English words mean as used by English speakers and writers. In most cases, their
definitions are far afield from what Hebrew and Greek words meant to the biblical
authors who used them.

Here's an English definition of love, in case you are wondering: "an intense feeling of deep affection." To be sure, *The New Oxford American Dictionary* is a repu-
table authority, but we need sometimes to remind ourselves that Jesus, Paul, Peter,
and others were not speaking English. They were first-century Jews, so we need to
get back to their world to understand how the word *love* was used in that world.
What did *love* mean at the time the Bible was being composed?

After writing *The Jesus Creed*, I began to work on defining love because I
wanted to settle it in my mind. Teaching courses where we discussed love forced me
to think through the term, which led me to the starting point. To define love *we
must go to the source of love — God*. God, the Bible tells us, *is* love. So to understand
what the Bible means by love, we need to *watch God love*. After reading the Bible
through with this conviction in mind, I have landed on this definition of love. *Love
is a rugged commitment to be with someone, for someone, as we journey in the transformation unto Christlikeness.*

Notice four elements in this brief definition. First, love is a *rugged commitment.* God expresses his love first and foremost by forming a covenant with humans— especially with Abraham in the twelfth and fifteenth chapters of Genesis. This covenant is in essence a promise that God will create a redeemed people who will be God's gift of blessing to the entire world. The term *covenant* is what I have in mind when I say "rugged commitment," and I use the word *rugged* because God's relationship with Abraham, with Abraham's descendants (Israel), and with the church is a far cry from constant joy and intimacy. There are good days for God's people (when they live faithfully) and bad days (when they choose to live apart from God). So God's covenant is a rugged commitment.

Wesley Hill, a professor who authored a significant book on love, points out that commitment is necessary if we are to make sense of love, or what he calls "spiritual friendship." He recounts author Maggie Gallagher's two kinds of relationships. One says, *You're mine because I love you,* and the second says, *I love you because you're mine.* Some of our relationships—such as the first of the two—rely exclusively on emotional bonding to carry the relationship through. We see this in some kinds of friendships. Others, however, are based on a promise: I love you because you're mine. The first type is based on "because I have love for you" and the second "because you're mine."

God's love is the "because you're mine" kind of love. Wesley has explained it like this:

> We are bound to each other, and therefore I love you. You may still bore me
> or wound me or otherwise become unattractive, but that doesn't mean I'll
> walk away. You're not mine because I love you; I love you because you're—
> already, and always—mine. We've made promises to each other; we've
> committed to each other, in the sight of our families and our churches, and in
> the strength of those vows, I will, God willing, go on loving you.[2]

In a note he then quotes Dietrich Bonhoeffer: "It is not your love that upholds marriage, but from now on it is marriage that upholds your love." God's kind of love, the kind of covenant God has made with us, is first and foremost a commitment to another person. And because personal commitments will encounter challenges, I add the further description that the personal commitment in love is rugged. (Most people are nodding in agreement, especially parents of teens.)

The second element of love is found in a preposition, *with*. God chooses to make a rugged commitment to us by choosing to be with us. God chooses to be *present*. God is present with Adam and Eve, and then God is present with Abraham by appearing in a smoking pot. God is present with Israel in the mobile tabernacle, and then God is present in the temple of Solomon when God's glory fills the temple. But God's presence is connected to the ruggedness of the commitment. At times, Israel's unfaithfulness forces God's blessed presence to withdraw from the temple. Meanwhile, God's covenant commitment remains secure.

That commitment-of-presence becomes a Person in the New Testament. The Gospel of Matthew tells us that Jesus—the one born in the long line anticipating the kingdom of God—is Immanuel, that is, God *with* us. If there is any place in the Bible that proves that love is a commitment of presence, it is in the use of the name *Immanuel* for Jesus.

In John 14, we read that Jesus promised he would send the Spirit to be his alter ego's *presence*. Jesus ascended, but the Spirit is God "with" us. This theme of God's love as a commitment to be with us becomes finally complete in the last vision of the Bible.

> And I heard a loud voice from the throne saying, "Look! God's dwelling place
> is now among the people, *and he will dwell with them.* They will be his
> people, and God himself *will be with them* and be their God."*

God's former "presence," as we have seen, was in heaven with the angels and archangels. But we read later in Revelation 21 that heaven and earth are joined, and God now establishes his permanent presence in the new heavens and the new earth with his people. To love, then, is to make a rugged commitment to be *with* someone. That's how God loves us.

---

* Revelation 21:3

The third term is *for*. When Revelation says in the quote above that "They will be his people, and God himself will be with them and be their God," the author is using important language—covenant language. This is the language that seals the deal in a covenant. It means "I've got your back; I'm on your side; I'm your warrior, your protector, your lover, your friend, and your God—now and forever." God, then, is our advocate. Love is a rugged commitment to be with someone in a way that communicates at the deepest level imaginable that we are *for* that person.

The fourth term in the Bible's definition of love is radically different from what the English dictionary offers in a definition of love. The fourth biblical word is about the direction of God's love: that is, it is *unto*. God loves us so that we can be transformed "unto" his treasured, holy, and loving community. God is holy and his love for us is an "unto" kind of holiness. God's holiness moves us forward and makes us holy; God is love and his love for us has direction and makes us loving. Put differently, union with God has *direction* and thus *is inevitably transformative.*

English dictionaries focus on the emotional depth and thrill of various kinds of unions with others. This understanding puts all the energy for creating and maintaining love on us. But the Bible takes us much deeper and much further because the Bible's sense of love has God as its source. With God, love can have direction. That is, in the Bible love has a goal; it has—to use the technical term—a *teleology.* Love is not tolerance or deciding to put up with one another or doing our best to get along. Love, if it is Christian love, leads to mutual growth into Christlikeness. That is its goal.

And this brings us back to angels. What do the four elements of love have to do with angels? Everything. They are sent by a God of love on a mission of love. The process of accomplishing the goal of love—which is our transformation—is highly likely to introduce major disruptions into our lives. Author and Episcopal priest Martha Sterne has observed:

> So the real job of angels is to pass hard and living good news on. Sometimes they show up in a conversation, or in a dream, or in a moment on a bus, or most often for me in the checkout line at the grocery store. They are more

likely to stir up the spirit than to smooth things down. Angels can be downright irritating since angels are in the business of startling people with the Holy and thus jump-starting people to come alive in the Spirit.[3]

God is a loving God who sends his angels to us for our redemptive transformation into humans who love God and who love others.

Now to Love and the Angels

At this point, two truths need to be observed: God is love, and God's mission for angels expresses that love. These lines express the core of the Bible's teaching about angels:

> God is Love.
> > All that God does is loving.
> > God sends angels to us because God loves us.
> > Love is a rugged commitment to be *With*,
> > to be *For* us, so that we can
> > progress *Unto* Christlikeness.
>
> > Angels are sent to express God's love
> > by being God's presence with us,
> > by being God's presence for us, and
> > to lead us into the redemption of Christlikeness.
>
> > Angels can't do anything for God that is not loving because the God who sends them and the God they obey is the God Who Is Love. They are agents of God's love.

We will turn now to how angels "pastor" us by loving us out of God's great love. We will see that they express God's "with-ness" and God's "for-ness" and God's "unto-ness." That is, they are God's presence with us, they are God's advocates for us, and they are God's transformative agents in our world for the sake of our redemption.

ANGELS CONFIRM GOD'S PRESENCE

Most Christians have had at least one moment when they wished God would just show up. What if he were to break through the barrier, say something aloud, or make himself so blatantly obvious that all doubts would disappear? In other words, while we are reasonably but sometimes wobbly confident that God loves us, we still would like unmistakable signs of God's *with-ness.*

Indications of God's presence may be stored in our memory from the past, perhaps from the days of our conversion, from a sermon that shook us to the core, from reading a book, from a time in prayer or solitude, or even from spending time in nature. Those experiences, while still valued, can crumble into a desire for a strong sense of God's sheer presence yet again.

We believe God is with us, and we can look at two Bible passages that make this truth clear and simple. First, God said the following to Joshua:

> No one will be able to stand against you all the days of your life. As I was
> with Moses, so I will be with you; I will never leave you nor forsake you. Be
> strong and courageous, because you will lead these people to inherit the land
> I swore to their ancestors to give them. *

---

* Joshua 1:5–6

That applied to the ancient heroes Joshua and Moses. But what about God's love and presence in the New Testament? Did not Jesus say these words?

And surely I am with you always, to the very end of the age. *

The essential redemptive promise from Abraham to the new heavens and the new earth is that God is *with us*. We believe that, but sometimes we want to experience it more tangibly. God's love means God is committed to be with us, and therefore God is all around us in ways we cannot see. God is present just behind the veil that shields us from his utter presence in the heavens. Angels express God's presence with us in love. I would suggest that the presence of angels is a tangible reality.

Angel or God?

In a scene by the trees of Mamre, described in the book of Genesis, Abraham and Sarah entertained three visitors. Every reader asks this question: Were the visitors humans or angels, or were they God in three persons? To help clear up the confusion, I would draw our attention to this: spirits on mission from God are angels of God's presence. As the pillar of cloud and pillar of fire were the presence of God to the children of Israel in the wilderness, as the tabernacle and the temple especially were where God dwelt among his people, and as Jesus was the express image of God among us, so angels are a visible encounter with the presence of God. They are not independent spirits showing up wherever and whenever they choose. No, they are spirits sent on mission to humans, and one thing they communicate is the presence of God.

Genesis 18 begins with these words: "The LORD† appeared to Abraham near the great trees of Mamre." In the very next sentence we read, "Abraham looked up and saw three *men*." Was it three men or was it the LORD?

Abraham and the visitors have a conversation, then Abraham scurries off to get a meal ready. A bit later we have this: "Then the LORD said to Abraham." And later,

---

* Matthew 28:20
† In English translations, *LORD* is used to translate the Hebrew divine name (*YHWH* or *Yahweh*), while *Lord* is used to translate *Adonai*. The English word *God* is the translation of *El* or *Elohim*.

the "*men* got up to leave" so Abraham walked on the path with them. Soon, however, the language shifts again. "The LORD" begins to consider whether to reveal to Abraham what can happen to Sodom if it does not repent and chooses to tell Abraham. When the *men* "turned away and went toward Sodom," Abraham "remained standing before the LORD." The two of them discuss how many righteous people need be present for the LORD to preserve the city. The story ends: "When the LORD had finished speaking with Abraham, he left, and Abraham returned home."*

In our confusion we ought to learn a colossal idea from the Bible: God appears in various forms, he becomes present in a multitude of ways, and *each* of these manifestations is *the presence of God*. The three men-visitors were the presence of God just as the LORD talking with Abraham was the presence of God.[1]

Perhaps we need to be more alert to the hum of angels in the unexpected visitor who appears briefly and then is gone suddenly. That presence is an expression of God's love. Here again are the central lines about angels in the Bible:

> God is Love.
>> All that God does is loving.
>> God sends angels to us because God loves us.
>> Love is a rugged commitment to be *With*,
>> to be *For* us so that we can
>> progress *Unto* Christlikeness.
>
>> Angels are sent to express God's love
>> by being God's presence with us,
>> by being God's presence for us, and
>> to lead us into the redemption of Christlikeness.

ANGEL ON FIRE

Moses encountered God in a drama designed to demonstrate God's presence

---

* Genesis 18:13–33

and to reveal the redemptive name of God to Moses.* Moses was minding a flock on the "far side of the wilderness" when he got to Mount Sinai (or Horeb). He was shocked to see a fire in a bush, which the Bible tells us was the "angel of the LORD." Curious, Moses approached the burning bush, and as he got close, God instructed him to remove his shoes for he was now standing on holy ground. At this moment God renewed his previous covenant promise, this time with Moses. "I am the God of your father, the God of Abraham, the God of Isaac and the God of Jacob."

What happened next is perhaps the Bible's deepest secret: God revealed his *name* to Moses. And God's name is one of eternal, redemptive presence. Here are the Bible's words:

> God said to Moses, "I AM WHO I AM. This is what you are to say to the Israelites: 'I AM has sent me to you.'"

As the narrative flows from Exodus all the way through to the end of Revelation, we learn that YHWH as God's name *means*

1. God is the all-encompassing Life-God,
2. this Life-God explicitly promises to be eternally present,
3. this Life-God rescues or redeems,
4. this Life-God abounds in love and forgiveness and justice, and
5. this Life-God becomes incarnate in Jesus.

If you ever wonder if God is present, think about the angel of the burning bush who anticipates Jesus, God incarnate, and you can see that the God who is present in angels is the God who becomes incarnate in Jesus. I am convinced, then, that angels anticipate the coming of Jesus. And that means I'm also convinced that wherever Jesus is, angels also are present.

To be sure, most of us never see angels present in settings that we connect to Jesus: worship, the Lord's table, the reading of Scripture, gathering with other believers. So instead of looking for apparitions, we need perhaps to readjust our ears to

---

* Exodus 3:1–14

hear the hum of God's angels sent to us in all the ways God reveals himself to us in Christ. The next section will show this.

ANGELS LURKING

Baldheaded Elisha was one of Israel's greatest prophets. He succeeded the first major prophet, Elijah, and received Elijah's very special kind of blessing. Elijah tossed his cloak over Elisha to designate him as his successor, and when Elijah was miraculously raptured into heaven, the cloak Elijah left behind became Elisha's, filled as it was with Elijah's power. Elisha was a man of God, mighty in miracles that included providing water and oil and food, as well as healing others of leprosy. He, too, learned to detect the hum of angels.*

Elisha was gifted by God with supernatural knowledge about a war the king of Aram wanted to wage against Israel. But the plans of the king of Aram failed because Elisha, in touch with special knowledge from God, informed Israel's king of the king of Aram's designs. Aram's king became furious and mistakenly assumed there must be a traitor in his own ranks. But he was told by a servant that Elisha was hearing the king's words, even when spoken in his own bedroom. So the king sent troops to capture the prophet.

Early one morning, Elisha's servant spotted the troops and warned Elisha of imminent disaster. Here is how Elisha responded to his servant (my italics, notice the theme of God's presence in the angels): "Don't be afraid," the prophet answered. "Those *who are with us* are more than those who are with them."

The servant must have looked around and wondered whom Elisha was referring to. The servant saw Elisha and himself and surely had no idea who "those who are with us" were. So Elisha prayed for his servant's eyes to be opened to see through the thin surface that separates this world from the world just beyond us.

Here is the important point about the presence of angels: *just because we don't see them doesn't mean they aren't present.* If we are listening we may well hear the

---

* All are found in 1 Kings 19:16–21 and 2 Kings 2–8; citations in what follows are from 2 Kings 6:16–17, 23.

hum of angels. So God opened Elisha's servant's eyes to see what one scholar has called "echoes of angels" that assumed the forms of chariots and horses.[2] Then the LORD opened the servant's eyes, and he looked and saw the hills full of horses and *chariots of fire* all around Elisha.

The chariots of fire mentioned in this verse echo the fire in the burning bush of Moses, but by all accounts what the servant saw was an army of God's angels. (Angels often are called "hosts" or "armies" in the Bible.) Also keep in mind that one type of angel, a *seraph,* means "fire." It's not a stretch to see a fiery army of seraph angels as God's special presence. Maybe we should pray to see beyond the thin veil that obscures the supernatural world God has created.

What happened after the opening of the servant's eyes? After the LORD answered Elisha's prayer and struck his enemies blind, Elisha led those who wanted to capture him to a city in Samaria, where he gave them food and drink and then sent them back to their king. The result: "The bands from Aram stopped raiding Israel's territory." Elisha gave his servant an opportunity to see the surprising presence of angels as messengers sent by God on a mission to deliver to God's people the graces of protection and redemption.

ANGELS ABOUNDING

We can't look at each angel incident in the Bible, so here's a list of angel appearances that remind us God is present even when we're not aware it is happening. I'll put my conviction about the constant presence of angels into a contorted sentence: the exceptions to God's absence *in the many appearances of angels* are a reminder of *God's presence* when the angels appear to be absent! I hope this makes as much sense to you as it does to me. God is present, and we dare not let the absence of *awareness* of angels in our personal lives make us think God is absent.

I begin with Jesus and the angels.

- When Mary was chosen to be mother of the Messiah, the angel Gabriel appeared to her.

- When Jesus was born, angels sounded the songs of glory.
- When Joseph was chosen to be father of the Messiah, the angel (Gabriel?) revealed the name of the boy about to be born: *Jesus.*
- When Jesus was threatened by the powers of Jerusalem, an angel told Joseph to take the family to Egypt.
- When their time in Egypt was over, an angel told Joseph to take the family back to the Holy Land.
- When Jesus had undergone his ordeal of temptation, the angels attended to him.
- John's Gospel tells us that believers would see heaven open up and angels descending on and ascending from Jesus, the Son of Man.
- When Jesus was tested to the limit of his capacities in Gethsemane, angels attended to him.
- When Jesus was raised from the dead, angels announced the resurrection.
- When Jesus ascended, angels informed the men from Galilee what had just happened.

Before Jesus was born, at his birth, at major moments in his life, at his resurrection, and at his return to the Father, there were angels. I don't want to turn our attention away from exalted glory of Jesus himself, and I don't want to suggest we are somehow a parallel to Jesus. Nor am I saying "as with Jesus, so with us." I'm not saying that angels attend us from before our birth until our final entrance into God's presence. But I will say this: *Christians are in Christ.* Because angels attend to Jesus at all times and because we are "in" Christ, we participate in the angels' presence with Jesus.

We can now take one more heart-stirring step: the entirety of our life is bathed in that angelic presence because we are in Christ.

If love is about a rugged commitment of presence—to be with someone—then God's love for Christ abounds in messages of presence in the abundance of angels. That same love, then, is directed toward all those who are in Christ! This abundant evidence of God's love for us in the life of Christ helps explain the abundant presence of angels in the early church.

- Arrested by the authorities for their preaching and healing, the apostles were delivered from prison by an angel of the Lord.
- Philip was guided by an angel, and he evangelized the Ethiopian eunuch.
- Both Cornelius, a Gentile God-fearer, and Peter, an apostle, encountered an angel. The encounters brought the two men together so Peter could tell Cornelius about Jesus.
- An angel rescued Peter from a prison cell.
- In the midst of a storm on the Mediterranean, an angel appeared to the apostle Paul to assure him that no one would perish in the storm and that he was destined to stand trial as a Christian before Caesar.
- The apostle John wrote the book of Revelation as a result of an angel's revelation.
- We are told in Revelation that each of the seven churches has an angel looking over it.
- One event after another in the visions of John in Revelation involves angels announcing and carrying out the mission of God. Angels are mentioned in Revelation more than fifty times.

Just beyond a thin veil at the edge of the physical world is another world far richer, far deeper, and far more inhabited. That world is filled with the hum of angels. At times, God pulls back the curtain for a moment, and we have a chance to observe that God's very presence is surrounded by thousands and thousands of angels. They also are a sacrament of God's love for us.

HOW CAN WE KNOW?

I now return to a theme introduced at the beginning of this chapter. The situation at the trees of Mamre was confusing. Three visitors arrived, and Abraham showed them hospitality. Were they men or were they angels or was it the LORD? The Bible makes clear that God was present, but the shifting back and forth between the passage's references to three men and then to God is confusing for most of us. Perhaps that confusion gives us an opportunity for learning. Our wonder might teach us to think that angels are more present than we think. We need to become more sensitive to whomever is in our presence. Centuries after Jacob the patriarch, the writer of Hebrews surely was thinking of Abraham when he instructed his readers with these words: "Do not forget to show hospitality to strangers, for by so doing some people have shown hospitality to angels without knowing it."

Those we think are humans might be angels, and angels are the presence of God, and God becomes present as a sign of his love for us!

But how can we know? Peter Kreeft's book on angels asks this question, and here is his answer: "If the angel is not wearing a human disguise, *you'll know!*" But, he continues, "If he is wearing a human disguise, you won't know he's an angel if he doesn't want you to." Then he reminds us: "Angels are smarter than we are."[3]

There you go. It's wiser to be aware of the presence of God in angels than to think angels show up only in neon lights. At times they appear to be humans. Perhaps we need to back down from our question about how we can know. Instead, we can ask ourselves why we ask that question. Do we wonder how we can know if it's an angel because our ears are so filled with the noise of modernity that we are unable to hear the ever-present hum? (I think so.)

Who knows, maybe the person you'd never seen on the bus before was a spirit clothed in a business suit and riding the bus on mission. Perhaps the woman at the swimming pool who conversed briefly with you was an angel sent from God to keep you on mission. Perhaps the person sitting in church, whom you had not seen before, was an angel checking out the church in a way that reminded you of what God wants to happen in this world.

"Who knows?" is a sharp enough question to keep us alert to the reality that God sends angels on mission to keep us on mission. Behind the "who knows?" is a deeper truth: God loves you, God sends angels, and God wants you to know that he sends these angels because of his love and grace for you.

---

* Hebrews 13:2

ANGELS SENT TO REDEEM

Love is not simply a feeling, a wish, or a hope. It is a rugged commitment to another person. If there is no commitment, there is no love. At the heart of that commitment is presence, that is, being with another person. It means being physically present in the routines of life, conversing about what matters most, discussing plans and failures and hopes. The Bible's best news is that God chooses to spend time with us in a number of ways, and one of those ways is by sending angels to us. God's presence creates our redemption. The angels are sent on mission from God to us to nudge us toward redemption.

ANGELS PROTECT US FOR OUR REDEMPTION

In Eden, Adam and Eve overreached their calling and chose to eat what God prohibited. In choosing to do what God said not to do, they decided they'd rather be gods and goddesses than servants of God. Their disaster created the ultimate elephant in the room: that tree. With the Tree of Life continuing to offer its ambrosia of immortality to the now-fallen Adam and Eve, God decided to send them into exile. Their exit was an act of grace on God's part.

Here is what the Bible says at the end of that story, beginning with God's pondering what should be done with Adam and Eve:

And the LORD God said, "The man has now become like one of us, knowing good and evil. He must not be allowed to reach out his hand and take also from the tree of life and eat, and live forever."*

Two verses later we read that God lovingly and redemptively takes surprisingly strong measures to make sure the humans don't eat from the Tree of Life.

After he drove the man out, he placed on the east side of the Garden of Eden cherubim and a flaming sword flashing back and forth to guard the way to the tree of life. †

My guess is that the first time you read the Bible, you either skipped over this verse about angels (or cherubim) or you read it and saw it as surprising. Before long you were onto Cain and Abel and Noah and the flood and didn't think again about the cherubim and the flaming sword guarding the way to the tree of life.

Or perhaps you read it long ago and have forgotten entirely about the cherubs in Eden or, perhaps instead, you read it and have long wondered, *What were those angels doing?* or *Why did God post angel sentries on the far side of Eden?* God set up the cherubs to protect Adam and Eve from being locked eternally in a sinful condition. Instead, God became present in the angels. He prevented the first people he created, and by extension the rest of us, from returning to the tree. He does this so we can enjoy final redemption.

The cherubs mentioned in this account are winged angelic beings that sometimes wield fiery, revolving swords to protect sacred items so humans will not partake.[1] In some ancient Middle Eastern art, the parallels to cherubs are human-headed winged lions, on the order of griffins and sphinxes, and are a long way from the tamed, chubby cherubs of Christian art. Cherubs are sent from God to protect us for the sake of our redemption. Bill Arnold, an expert on the book of Genesis, describes life for all of us after Eden: "To be human is thus to live in a balance between boundless potentiality and a 'grounded' realism that life is short."[2] Notice what

---

* Genesis 3:22
† Genesis 3:24

Arnold says about you and me: we have "boundless potentiality." How so? The message of redemption is that angels are sent to protect us from an eternal attachment bond to mortality so we can discover immortality in redemption.

Which is to say, *From the moment we sinned, God began our redemption. And from that same beginning, God plotted angels to be present to protect us so we can find redemption.*

ANGELS ARE WITH US TO PROVIDE FOR OUR REDEMPTION

There is a Bible story that scares us and at the same time fills us with joy. The story draws us in though we may be covering our eyes, wondering why God would tell Abraham to do such a thing. And by the time the story's over, we are jumping up and down in relief. When Gil Smith read this passage in our church one Sunday, the story so overcame him he teared up. If you are a good reader, you will too. I'll review the story.

God promised Abram and Sarai, soon to be called Abraham and Sarah, enough babies that someday their descendants would outnumber the stars. As the years moved along, they looked at each other time and again to say, "No babies!" Then they voiced their concerns to God with "Where are the babies, God?" The Lord was "gracious" and did "what he had promised."* Which means in their old age, Abraham and Sarah had a baby boy named *Yitzak,* or Isaac. All their hopes were focused in that one son. He was the bridge to God's fulfilling all God's promises for a great seed.†

This is a wonderful story until . . .

Some time later God tested Abraham. He said to him, "Abraham!"

"Here I am," he replied.

Then God said, "Take your son, your only son, whom you love—
Isaac—and go to the region of Moriah. Sacrifice him there as a burnt offering on a mountain I will show you."

---

* Genesis 21:1
† The following quotations are from Genesis 22.

It takes no imagination to picture the way Abraham and Sarah would have responded. It was Abraham's first step toward Moriah that overwhelms us. There is no indication that he hesitated, lamented, or interceded on behalf of his son of promise. "Early the next morning," the Bible tells us, he "got up and loaded his donkey." He took along two servants and Isaac, who is his one and only son, his beloved. The next line disturbs me every time I read the text: "When he had cut enough wood for the burnt offering, he set out . . ."

Three days later he sees Moriah and tells the servants to stay where they are. He and Isaac will proceed unaccompanied to do what God had said.

But Abraham seemingly knows our worries, so he drops hope to his servants. Before going on ahead, he said, "We will worship and then *we* will come back to you." I like that word *we* with its hint of hope. Still, hope-on-the-way-to-child-sacrifice confuses the story. Confusion is what is supposed to happen to the attentive reader. Isaac expresses our confusion when he asks his aged father this chilling question: "The fire and wood are here, but where is the lamb for the burnt offering?" Abraham drops another hint of faith-based hope: "God himself will provide *the lamb* for the burnt offering, my son." Isaac trusts his believing-in-hope father.

What was supposed to happen now happens.

> When they reached the place God had told him about, Abraham built an
> altar there and arranged the wood on it. He bound his son Isaac and laid him
> on the altar, on top of the wood. Then he reached out his hand and took the
> knife to slay his son.

This is the low point of Genesis, for sure, and along with God's people in Egypt suffering under Pharaoh, one of the low points of the entire Old Testament. Lay it next to the day Jesus died, and you get a picture of the darkness covering the whole land.

And now, the redemptive interruption. Abraham was surprised by the loving, redemptive presence of an angel.

> The angel of the LORD called out to him from heaven, "Abraham!
> Abraham!"

Never was a father more attentive to the presence of God. "Here I am!" Then the best words imaginable, turning the scene from a tragedy reflective of Good Friday to the overwhelming joy and celebration of Easter:

"Do not lay a hand on the boy. Do not do anything to him. Now I know that you fear God."

The special messenger from God, the Angel of the LORD, had done his work. The angel tested, watched, and stopped Abraham.

The Bible continues with great news. The news is that Abraham's son will be redeemed by a *specially provided sacrifice.*

Abraham looked up and there in a thicket he saw a ram caught by its horns. He went over and took the ram and sacrificed it as a burnt offering instead of his son. So Abraham called that place The LORD Will Provide. And to this day it is said, "On the mountain of the LORD it will be provided."

One doesn't have to be a theologian to see what happened on the mountain. God asked for Abraham's son, Abraham was so in tune with God that he offered his son to God and continued to hope. God intervened in the loving redemptive presence of an angel that provided a "ram" for the sacrifice.[3] And this story becomes the prototypical story of Jesus's death for our redemption on Good Friday.

This act turns at a dark corner in history toward a path in the light of redemption. In a day when the people surrounding Abraham were sacrificing their firstborn sons to the gods and goddesses to protect the people from evil, sickness, disease, famine, and war, an angel's sudden presence interrupts and surprises the assumptions and practices of the ancient world. The angel disrupted everything with a whole new way of grace. Instead of sacrificing their sons, Abraham's descendants would only "wound" their sons with circumcision. In the place of offering children on altars, the angel supplied an animal. God softened the culture toward redemption, grace, life, and hope instead of superstition, death, and fear. And he sent this way of redemption on the wings of an angel.

God will now be known as *YHWH-YIREH,* which is to say, God will see to the provision and redemption. Many simply translate the new name as "God will provide." God did provide, and then God promised Abraham a second time that his progeny would make up multitudes.

The story ends with a wonderful understatement: "Then Abraham returned to his servants, and *they* set off together for Beersheba." All of them. Abraham, happy beyond words. Isaac, relieved to be alive and no longer wrestling with confusion. And the servants, who must have asked about the worship event on the mountain. They all now know God as YHWH-YIREH, and they learned about God from an angel—an angel sent for redemption.

8

ANGELS TEACH FROM
THE BEGINNING

The Bible challenges the flat cosmology of moderns with a thick cosmology. It is filled not only with what we can see (stars, planets, the gravitational wave, plants, trees, rivers, and mountains) and what we know from experience (humans inhabiting the globe, families, love, society, politics, peace, and war), but also with invisible spiritual beings. If our flat modern cosmology says, *There is no god because I can't touch God* or *There are no angels because I can't demonstrate them in a laboratory,* the Bible's cosmology says, *God made it all and there's more than you can see. Open your eyes to wonder!*

Modern people can be uncomfortable with the confidence shown by biblical figures in the invisible world. Comfortable or not, moderns can see that the Bible reveals God and a cosmos inhabited—most of the time unseen, to be sure—by supernatural beings. When Bruce Gordon summed up his study of angels in the Renaissance, he had this to say of what the ordinary person then believed:

> In late medieval Europe the omnipresence of angels was not simply an acknowledged verity but a daily assurance and reminder of the transcendent God. . . . They could be certain of encountering angels at the

moments of death and of judgement, and in the heavenly court, but were less confident about precisely when these spiritual beings would intervene in their lives as protectors, advisors and bearers of God's revelation.[1]

Gordon wrote that angels sometimes are "advisors and bearers of God's revelation." God loves us enough to become present in angels in order to reveal deep truths. Angels are, as Karl Barth once astutely observed, "the originals of the prophets and apostles."[2]

An overview of the Bible shows that angels are involved in *every major moment* of God's revelation. This might surprise us, but think about this: they are present when God reveals and assures Abraham and Sarah of his promise, they are present when the law is given, they are present when the prophets speak and when they need further interpretation, and—as we will see later in this book—they surround Jesus from the beginning of his life to the end.

That's not all. They are all over the consummation of history that we read about in the book of Revelation. In this chapter and the next, we will look at three of these major moments of revelation: promise, law, and prophets.

Once again, let's recall the central teaching of the Bible about angels and notice where the angels, our teachers, fit in:

> God is Love.
>> All that God does is loving.
>> God sends angels to us because God loves us.
>> Love is a rugged commitment to be *With*,
>> to be *For* us so that we can
>> progress *Unto* Christlikeness.
>
>> Angels are sent to express God's love
>> by being God's presence *with* us *in teaching us*,
>> by being God's presence for us, and
>> to lead us into the redemption of Christlikeness.

ANGELS WITH US TODAY

Tracy Smith, director of Princeton University's Program in Creative Writing and winner of the 2012 Pulitzer Prize for poetry, told a story about her mother dying. It was the autumn after Smith had graduated from Harvard. She had been home with her mother for six weeks when an angel appeared to her mother. Here are Tracy's words (and words I italicized to draw attention to our focus):

> One night, my mother began talking to someone in a low voice. Though I knew the medications caused this, it always startled me, as if she could see through this world to the next, to the places where ghosts and angels sit and walk and gesture unseen among us. Very calmly, as if she were speaking to someone seated beside her on the bed, she said, "Yes, I know she will, if that's what she wants to do." My eyes filled with tears. I felt instinctively that she was talking about me.
>
> "Who is there *with you?*" I asked.
>
> Usually, she'd laugh and say a thing like, "Oh, this medicine has me confused." But this time she said, very clearly and now very much awake, "There are two angels sitting here, Tracy, and one of them just told me *you're going to become a writer.*"
>
> Jean and I must have asked her what they looked like, what else they'd said, but all I remember is the ensuing silence, the feeling that something powerful was there at her side. Did it mean she might live after all? Could the angels, or whoever had sent them, see to that? Or had they come to usher her away, to orient her to a new and altogether foreign realm?

The hum of angels permits me to believe that two angels, whose presence is noted by "with you," comforted that special mother with words that revealed where life would take Tracy Smith.[3] Perhaps you have entered such an aha moment when listening to a preacher, reading a stimulating book, absorbing a wondrous combination of words and sound in song, or engaging in conversation with a wise person.

Perhaps you, too, have sensed that we are being attended by angels sent from God to make sure we learn about God's love.

Angels reveal messages to us on earth. We see plenty of examples in the Bible, going back to God's original promise to Abraham, the promise of redemption.

ABRAHAM, THE PROMISE, AND THE ANGELS

The story begins when three nameless strangers appear to Abraham "in the heat of the day" when he was sitting near the great trees of Mamre.* As Moses relates the story, "the LORD appeared" but it was in the form of three men. Of the three men walking with Abraham toward Sodom, two continue on to disclose information to Lot, and they are said to be "angels."† So suggestive is the scene in this story that the great Russian iconographer Andrei Rublev turned the three angels into the three persons of the Trinity in his famous iconographic painting, *The Hospitality of Abraham* or *The Holy Trinity*. Similarly, the Jewish tradition, while not affirming the Christian belief in God as Trinity, names the three angels Michael, Gabriel, and Raphael.[4]

In the first scene, Abraham begs the three to stay for a meal. Abraham then tells Sarah to bake some bread, and he finds a young calf for his servant to prepare. The three visitors are presented a meal that includes curds and milk along with the calf. How angels eat is an interesting discussion. Judaism, Christianity, and Islam have their theories, but we don't know. One of the angels tells Abraham that Sarah will have a son in a year. When Sarah hangs an LOL sign in her heart, the LORD hears it and tells Abraham, and it leads to a family squabble.

The second scene: The LORD, by means of the visiting angels, discloses that Sodom will be destroyed. Then Abraham sees if he can negotiate with the LORD. He succeeds in getting the LORD to reconsider four times, each time reducing the number of righteous people required to be in Sodom to head off the LORD's destruction. Abraham wants his nephew Lot spared the judgment of God against the injustices and sins of Sodom. Eventually, Abraham gets God to promise that Sodom will not be destroyed if as few as ten righteous men can be found in the city.

---

* Genesis 18–19
† See Genesis 19:1.

Third scene: Two of the angels are commissioned to deliver divine disclosures to Lot. When Lot, seated in the gateway to the city, sees them, he offers them hospitality. The angels wanted to spend the night "in the square," but Lot convinces them it's safer to take shelter in his home. They enter his home and have a meal, but the men of Sodom bully Lot, indicating they want to have sex with his visitors. (This part of the story is beyond sickness.)

The bullying gets worse. The angels grab Lot and pull him back into the house. Then the angels, who suddenly become messengers of destruction, strike the gang of men with blindness. The angels reveal God's message to Lot: escape with your family for your own redemption. The violence and injustice were so bad God was about to destroy the city.

Lot's sons-in-law think the old man is unstable and choose to stay; Lot needs the angels themselves to grab his hand, along with the hands of his wife and his two daughters, before he can be convinced to abandon Sodom. Flee, the angels tell them, and don't look back. Lot asks the angels to let them flee to Zoar, and by the time he reaches Zoar, early in the morning, Sodom is burning. (Lot's wife famously looks back and turns into a pillar of salt.)

These scenes leave one tantalizing question after another on the table, none of which need to be resolved immediately. Our concern is this: God sometimes becomes present in angels to disclose divine secrets to his people, and this leads to their redemption. One more angel episode from the Old Testament will illustrate how angels are the very presence of a loving God's effective communication with humans, this time with Jacob.

JACOB, THE PROMISE, AND THE ANGEL

The patriarch Jacob journeyed to the hometown of Abram and Sarai, the obscure place called Harran, to find a wife from his own people. (He had refused to take a wife from among the Canaanites).* He spent the night in a place called Luz, and used a stone for a pillow. This was his dream:

---

* Genesis 28

He had a dream in which he saw a stairway resting on the earth, with its top
reaching to heaven, and the angels of God were ascending and descending on
it. There above it stood the LORD, and he said:

"I am the LORD, the God of your father Abraham and the God of Isaac.
I will give you and your descendants the land on which you are lying. Your
descendants will be like the dust of the earth, and you will spread out to the
west and to the east, to the north and to the south. All peoples on earth will
be blessed through you and your offspring. I am with you and will watch over
you wherever you go, and I will bring you back to this land. I will not leave
you until I have done what I have promised you."

When Jacob awoke from his sleep, he thought, "Surely the LORD is in
this place, and I was not aware of it." He was afraid and said, "How awesome
is this place! This is none other than the house of God; this is the gate of
heaven."

In a dream, angels appeared ascending and descending to Jacob with a surprising revelation: the Abraham promise is still on! The stairway to heaven symbolizes
back-and-forth communication between God in heaven with humans on earth.*
(Notice the pattern of "with me" references made in divine love in what follows.)

Then Jacob made a vow, saying, "If God will be *with me* and will watch over
me on this journey I am taking and will give me food to eat and clothes to
wear so that I return safely to my father's household, then the LORD will be
my God and this stone that I have set up as a pillar will be God's house, and
of all that you give me I will give you a tenth."

The next surprising divine disclosure made to Jacob has to do with a name, and
it occurred in one of the oddest and most significant events in the Bible. Again, an
angel became the presence of God and revealed the message of redemption.

Jacob was about to encounter his brother, Esau, from whom he stole the birthright

---

* See John 1:51.

to the family inheritance. Jacob's family and farm had grown tremendously, and he was moving the whole lot back to the Holy Land. But he feared Esau. So Jacob prayed and made promises and pleaded for protection. He chose to give an extravagant gift to his brother in the hope of calming the man down. He sent servants ahead with gifts, while he and his family stayed behind. (Surely I'm not the only one muttering "Coward!") After he sent his family across a stream, he remained behind.

So Jacob was left alone, and a man wrestled with him till daybreak. When the man saw that he could not overpower him, he touched the socket of Jacob's hip so that his hip was wrenched as he wrestled with the man. Then the man said, "Let me go, for it is daybreak."

But Jacob replied, "I will not let you go unless you bless me."

The man asked him, "What is your name?"

"Jacob," he answered.

Then the man said, "Your name will no longer be Jacob, but Israel, because you have struggled with God and with humans and have overcome."

Jacob said, "Please tell me your name."

But he replied, "Why do you ask my name?" Then he blessed him there.

So Jacob called the place Peniel, saying, "It is because I saw God face to face, and yet my life was spared."*

Jacob had spent that night alone with God, wrestling with God in the form of a man who was an angel. Jacob was wounded in the hip, blessed, and renamed. From that day on Jacob was called Israel, and his people became known as Israel. From that day on the limp was a sacrament of an angel's disclosure, a disclosure of what God wants the people of Israel to know.

Here are two major events, one involving Abraham and Lot and the other involving Jacob and Esau. Both events were attended powerfully by angels. Both involved the communication of God's enduring love for the world, so much that God established a family (Israel) whose mission it was to bless the entire world.

---

* Genesis 32

And not insignificantly, both events included angels, our teachers, revealing the redemptive message of the Bible: God promises to be with his people as the God who will redeem them because God loves those whom he has created. We can begin to adjust our ears, I am suggesting, to something new. When we are learning about God's grace and love, we can be confident that angels are present.

We began this chapter observing that angels participated in every major moment of revelation in the Bible, which we broke down into these themes: promises, law, prophets, and Jesus himself. Our next chapter continues the discussion by looking at the law and prophets. (We'll save the angels and Jesus for later chapters.)

ANGELS TEACH THE BIBLE'S BIG IDEAS

God communicated promise after promise to people such as Abraham and Sarah, Lot, and Jacob through angels. We cannot emphasize enough the importance of the Bible's promise theme, which begins in the twelfth chapter of Genesis. God promised Abraham—literally—the world. The promise is ratified three chapters later in a dramatic covenant ceremony; it is renewed with Moses and David. Later, the prophet Jeremiah predicted the renewal of the covenant in a new covenant, which was fulfilled in Jesus at the last supper.

The apostle Paul made a huge deal about God's original promises to Abraham, which opened the door for Paul's mission to include Gentiles in the new family of God, the church. Angels are connected to the grand promise of the Bible since they participated in the promises given to Abraham and to Jacob. Angels also are connected to God's laws, his instructions for how God's people are to live. Two of the most important words in the Bible are *promise* and *law,* and both are connected to angels.

MOSES, THE LAW, AND THE ANGELS

Angels participated in communicating the promise as well as in making known God's laws to Israel. It is unfortunate that Christians often look down their noses at the laws of Moses. Some say they are too primitive for life today. But that's like pretending computers were not anticipated by typewriters. Jesus and the apostles never dissed the law as primitive but instead held it up as God's good Word for God's people. When Jesus gave his famous Sermon on the Mount, he offered to his disciples nothing less than a kingdom version of the law of Moses, often called the Torah. The sermon's most striking words are "You have heard that it was said . . . But I tell you . . ." With those words as preamble, Jesus taught how his followers are to *fulfill* the law of Moses by following his instructions. When the apostle Paul taught Christians how to live, he told them if they learned to love others they'd be doing everything the Torah taught. He even said that those who live in the Spirit will accomplish a law-like life!* So for Jesus and the apostles, the law was a gift from God instructing God's people how to live.

The book of Psalms opens with a blessing on anyone "whose delight is in the law of the LORD." Another psalm says the commandments in the law are "more precious than gold." And in the famous chapter that sings the praise of God's gift of the Torah, we read these lines:

> Oh, how I love your law!
>> I meditate on it all day long.
> Your commands are always with me
>> and make me wiser than my enemies."†

There is a little secret about this precious law of Moses: it was hand (or wing!) delivered to Moses *by angels*. Here are some of the verses that show angels present with Moses as they revealed the Torah to him.‡

> He was in the assembly in the wilderness, *with the angel who spoke to him* on Mount Sinai, and with our ancestors; and he received living words to pass on to us.

---

* Romans 8:1–4, esp. verse 4
† Psalm 1:1–2; 19:10; 119:97–8
‡ Acts 7:38, 53; Galatians 3:19; Hebrews 2:2–3

You who have received the law that was *given through angels* but have not obeyed it.

Why, then, was the law given at all? It was added because of transgressions until the Seed to whom the promise referred had come. The law was *given through angels* and entrusted to a mediator [Moses].

For since *the message spoken through angels* was binding, and every violation and disobedience received its just punishment, how shall we escape if we ignore so great a salvation?

The Bible is a gift sent by God through angel messengers so we could know the will of God. We should respect the Book itself as having been delivered by God's special agents, the angels. This is God's revelation of how God wants God's people to live.

Let's back up to see the big picture again. God is love; our loving God communicates *with* us through the angels. Angels reveal what God wants us to know for our own redemption. The angels have been sent by God as our teachers. Everything we learn about promise and law comes through God's curious, caring, and obedient spirits, the angels.

And now we turn to the prophets.

DANIEL, PROTECTION, REVELATION, AND THE ANGELS

The prophet Daniel is both enigmatic and paradigmatic: he's a prophet stuffed full with riddles as well as the very model on which Jesus built his kingdom vision. Daniel offers parables and prophecies that require serious thinking to understand, and he spoke about a figure called the "son of man." So important was the son of man to Jesus that he used Daniel's son of man—as one notable Christian thinker called it—as his "job description."[1] We can be grateful to Jesus for explaining how "son of man" worked, but we might wish he had explained more of Daniel's sayings. Where did one prophet get such a strange combination of wildness and depth? The answer: from angels.

Angel No. 1

Nebuchadnezzar, one of the world's great egomaniacs who surely anticipated his geographic descendant Saddam Hussein, built an image of himself sixty cubits high and six cubits wide,* commanded everyone to worship his image, and threatened anyone who refused with a capital sentence. The execution would be carried out in a blazing furnace. Three Jewish leaders with names only the Sunday-school-raised children know (Shadrach, Meshach, and Abednego—which we renamed "shake the bed, make the bed, and to bed we go!")—refused to worship the image. They were summarily tossed into the furnace, the furnace was fired up to seven times its normal heat, and—no surprise to all but the new kid in Sunday school—an angel delivered them. The idolatrous King Nebuchadnezzar, the Bible tells us, saw not three men but four in the furnace, the additional one being the angel sent for protection. The king caved in and declared that Israel's God was too powerful to contest, and he threatened punishment for any who opposed Israel's great and mighty God. Subsequently, the three men were given a promotion.†

Angel No. 2

Darius, the king of Persia, realized Daniel was nothing short of an administrative genius. The king appointed him over the whole land. Politics being about power, some of Darius's other administrators were intensely jealous so they plotted to do Daniel in. They discovered that he, like the three men mentioned earlier, was a worshiper of Israel's God. He worshiped that God alone, and he prayed on his roof three times per day. The plotters convinced Darius to ban prayer to other gods, and not knowing what this would mean for Daniel, the king got trapped in their machinations.‡

At this point in the book of Daniel, the punishment has changed. Instead of a blazing furnace, a den with hungry lions is the method of execution. The king sealed the den with his signet ring, found no rest for his soul all night, hurried the next morning to the den to see if God had rescued the man he prized so highly, and dis-

---

* A cubit is a little less than two feet.
† Daniel 3
‡ Daniel 6

covered what (one suspects) he hoped would be the case. The king yelled into the den to see if Daniel was there, and here are Daniel's words:

> May the king live forever! My God *sent his angel,* and he shut the mouths of the lions. They have not hurt me, because I was found innocent in his sight. Nor have I ever done any wrong before you, Your Majesty.*

Forget the lions and think about the angel that sealed their mouths.

These two stories set up what comes next. Daniel saw visions with parables inside of parables and odd images on top of odd images. They could not be understood without revelation. Which leads us to Angel No. 3.

Angel No. 3

After seeing the bizarre and threatening images of the four beasts and that great and glorious indication of the coming Messiah, the Son of Man, Daniel admitted he couldn't take it all in:

> I, Daniel, was troubled in spirit, and the visions that passed through my mind disturbed me. I approached one of those standing there [= an angel] and asked him the meaning of all this.
>
> So he told me and gave me the interpretation of these things: "The four great beasts are four kings that will rise from the earth. But the holy people of the Most High will receive the kingdom and will possess it forever—yes, for ever and ever."†

The appearance of an angel to instruct Daniel happens more than once in the prophecies of Daniel, but this one instance is plenty: Daniel sees a vision from God but needs instruction, and God sends an angel to Daniel to interpret the vision.

Time to sum it up: angels are ever present and involved in *every major moment* of revelation. We see this happen with the *promise* of God to Abraham to bless the

---

* Daniel 6:21–22
† Daniel 7:15–18

whole world with redemption; with the *law* that leads to our redemption; and with the *prophets* who reveal how redemption works and how it will work. The angels are our teachers. Those caring, curious angels, we need to see, are at work to teach us the message of redemption.

The Bible came to us from God through angels. Every time you read the Bible, the angels are attending and nudging and guiding and suggesting and prompting you to hear about God's love and that God's aim is your redemption. Angels are not Cupid-like little arrow-carrying cuties but curious, compassionate, and mission-minded agents of God. The Bible is attended by the hum of angels.[2]

10

ANGELS BRING GOD'S COMFORT

Some consider angels in a historical context, comparing them to ancient Middle Eastern spiritual beings, while others consider them philosophically and ponder what they are and whether they have will, intellect, and personhood. These questions miss the most important point: angels are *agents of redemption* sent by God to communicate God's love for us and God's desire for our redemption. As the God of love, God has made a rugged commitment—a covenant—with us to be present, to be our advocate, and to transform us into Christlike people. Angels are an expression of the loving presence of God.

Sometimes they are sent to comfort us, as can be seen in this story of a friend of a friend who passed it on to me (with the name changed):

It was the night of my daughter Jesse's accident, and all my family had left the hospital as we were told that Jesse and the baby were fine. Shortly after everyone left Jesse's placenta erupted, and she was immediately taken away for a C-section at only thirty weeks pregnant.

I was alone in her room when a nurse named Mary came in to sit with me. She helped me call my family back to the hospital, and she continued to sit with me until they arrived. We talked about my daughter and my granddaughter, she comforted me, and I was overcome with peace at a time when I should have been overcome with fear.

She informed me when my family arrived. (Actually, she didn't leave the room, she just knew they were there, though I didn't realize that until sometime later.) I went to the waiting room, and there was my family, just getting out of the elevator.

The next night I went back to thank Nurse Mary for sitting with me. I was told there was no Nurse Mary and no nurse fit her description.

Jesse's mother believes she was comforted by an angel. So do I.

Have you ever wondered how God decides when to send an angel or how he decides which angel to send? Is there a heavenly committee that decides these things? Or are all the angels (metaphorically) squatting in starting blocks waiting for the mission gun to go boom, and off one or more of them go? One of the more interesting features about angels in the Bible is that they are (at least at times) sent following the decision of a divine council. Before we get to the angels' mission of comfort, let's look at heaven's divine council, or what we might call heaven's boardroom.

GOD AND THE BOARDROOM OF HEAVEN

In the opening chapters of Genesis, God speaks of "us." "Let us make mankind in our image, in our likeness." After Adam and Eve chose to do what God expressly prohibited, God said, "The man has now become like one of us."* A few chapters later, in the famous Tower of Babel event, God said, "Let us go down and confuse their language."† Who is this Us? We know God, a singular deity. So who are the others that turn the singular into a plural Us?

Many Bible experts believe the Us is the divine council, that is, an assembly of supernatural beings who dwell in the divine presence and who, after a council meeting (metaphorically speaking), are sent on missions as angels. In the times of the Old Testament, a king gathered the pantheon of his chosen counselors for consultation and then bade them go on their way to accomplish his mission. The appearance in the Bible of a council-like pantheon surrounding God gave rise to all sorts of speculations among Jewish thinkers. (There is no better speculation than what Jewish phi-

---

* Genesis 1:26; 3:22
† Genesis 11:7

losophers and theologians engage in.) One of my favorites concerns an argument between angels about whether God ought to create humans (from a rabbinic source called *Midrash Rabbah* 8:5):

> Rabbi Simon said: "When the Holy One, blessed be He, came to create
> Adam, the ministering angels formed themselves into groups and parties,
> some of them saying, 'Let him be created,' while others urged, 'Let him not
> be created.' Thus it is written, 'Love and Truth fought together, Right-
> eousness and Peace combated each other.' [Psalm 85:11]: Love said, 'Let him
> be created, because he will dispense acts of love'; Truth said, 'Let him not be
> created, because he is compounded of falsehood'; Righteousness said, 'Let
> him be created, because he will perform righteous deeds'; Peace said, 'Let him
> not be created because he is full of strife.' . . .
>
> While the ministering angels were arguing with each other and disputing
> with each other, the Holy One, blessed be He, created him. God said to
> them, 'What can you avail? Man has already been made!' "[1]

Anything less than God, and angels are less than God, can get into arguments, so I don't put that element of this story into the world of legend and fiction. What this account illustrates is what is meant by a divine council. This *Midrash Rabbah* text is fun, but there are some reasons for us to think a little bit more about God's council of angels. Why? Because it is mentioned often in the Old Testament. There are very good examples of God's being depicted as engaged in heaven's High Council with the angels. The first one exhorts the angels in God's presence to praise him and the second speaks clearly of the council itself:

> Ascribe to the LORD, *you heavenly beings,*
>   ascribe to the LORD glory and strength.

> The heavens praise your wonders, LORD,
>   your faithfulness too, in the assembly of the holy ones.
> For who in the skies above can compare with the LORD?

> Who is like the LORD among the heavenly beings?
> *In the council of the holy ones* God is greatly feared;
>> he is more awesome *than all who surround him.*
> Who is like you, LORD God Almighty?
>> You, LORD, are mighty, and your faithfulness surrounds you.*

The prophet Micaiah said, "I saw the LORD sitting on his throne with *all the multitudes [or hosts] of heaven* standing around him on his right and on his left."† (I suspect many Bible readers think this kind of language is metaphor. Such an assumption overlooks the Bible's cosmology of a world filled with invisible beings.) There is something dramatic in this very special scene in the Bible, and so we must read on:

> And the LORD said, "Who will entice Ahab into attacking Ramoth Gilead
> and going to his death there?"
>> One suggested this, and another that. Finally, a spirit came forward,
> stood before the LORD and said, "I will entice him."
>> "By what means?" the LORD asked.
>> "I will go out and be a deceiving spirit in the mouths of all his prophets,"
> he said.
>> "You will succeed in enticing him," said the LORD. "Go and do it."‡

This divine council, once again, calls to mind the ancient pantheons as well as modern gatherings of members of Congress. That is, they are not all on the same page. God seemingly can summon all the spirits, all the supernatural beings, angels good and bad, into his presence for an assembly.[2] Perhaps I need to mention the opening scene of the book of Job, where Satan appears before God with the desire to destroy the man of God, Job, by taking everything from him. We need only mention this in order to fill out the picture of God's presence flooded with supernatural beings and not all of them good.

---

* Psalm 29:1; 89:5–8
† 1 Kings 22:19
‡ 1 Kings 22:20–22

This sketch of the divine council sets the stage for comprehending every angelic visitor in the Bible and history. They are spirits sent on mission by God to humans, and they are sent to keep us on mission. Just maybe there was a heavenly conversation that prompted God's decision to send angels on a specific mission. On a number of occasions, God sends angels on missions to comfort us. I observe three themes in angelic comfort: our earthly battles, our spiritual battles, and our uncertainties about the future as we face death.

Comfort in the earthly battle

The first three major human leaders of God's people who appear in the Bible are Abraham, Moses, and Joshua. Joshua succeeded Moses and was chosen by God to lead the wandering children of Israel across the Jordan River and into the land. Joshua was a leader among leaders. He led in battle as well as directing the people generally. Angels in the Bible can be fierce warriors. It is comforting to know God has an angelic commander with an army of mighty warriors fighting with us.

Joshua learned this as he approached the battlefield in the battle of Jericho. Joshua's forces were outmatched and outmanned, but they had supernatural help:

> Now when Joshua was near Jericho, he looked up and saw a man standing in front of him with a drawn sword in his hand. Joshua went up to him and asked, "Are you for us or for our enemies?"
>
> "Neither," he replied, "but as commander of the army of the LORD I have now come."*

Many of us would like to have heard the commander of the Lord's army say, "For you!" but that's not what he said. Before the battle was joined, the commander wanted Joshua to surrender himself to the Lord in worship as he realized he was standing on holy ground. And worship is what he did. Continuing now with the lines just cited:

---

* Joshua 5:13–15. Joshua 6 tells the story of Jericho's demise.

Then Joshua fell facedown to the ground in reverence, and asked him, "What message does my Lord have for his servant?"

The commander of the LORD's army replied, "Take off your sandals, for the place where you are standing is holy." And Joshua did so.*

Only when they take the posture of worshiping God does the Lord give Jericho to the people of Israel. It takes courage to walk up to a sword-armed stranger and ask if he is for you or against you. Joshua was a military leader, and he showed his courage again and again. We might not be entirely comfortable with his combined roles of covenant-people pastor and battlefield warrior, but that's where the Bible takes us to see an angel at work. The man reveals who he is to Joshua: commander of the army of YHWH! Joshua was in the presence of not a man but an angel sent from God.

This is an angel of revelation and comfort. His words are that God has given this city, Jericho, to the people of God. The account about Jericho ends with these words: "So the LORD was *with* Joshua, and his fame spread throughout the land." God is a God of love; to love is to make a rugged commitment to be "with" someone. God makes that kind of commitment, the presence of an angel, to Joshua.

Comfort in the spiritual battle

The Bible's cosmology is that God created the earth *and* the heavens. He populated earth with what we would call visible, earthly creatures, humans included. But he also made the heavens and populated the heavens with (what are to us) invisible, heavenly creatures. Not all the heavenly creatures are good. In fact, some are out to get us. They engage in battle to conquer all those who align themselves with Jesus. Call it what you want, but there is a cosmic battle going on.

The apostle Paul brought it to the fore when he wrote, "For our struggle is not against flesh and blood, but against the rulers, against the authorities, against the powers of this dark world and against the spiritual forces of evil in the heavenly realms."† We will look at this theme in chapter 18.

There is something of immense comfort in the Bible's descriptions of battles.

---

* Joshua 5:13–15; Joshua 6
† Ephesians 6:12

Not only has Christ conquered those powers* but there appears to be an archangel named Michael who has been assigned to the battle, and he fights for us. In the book of Revelation, we are given a revelation not only that the battle is on but that Michael *has won the battle for us.*

> Then war broke out in heaven. Michael and his angels fought against the dragon, and the dragon and his angels fought back. But he was not strong enough, and they lost their place in heaven. The great dragon was hurled down—that ancient serpent called the devil, or Satan, who leads the whole world astray. He was hurled to the earth, and his angels with him.†

So even if Michael was doing battle for Daniel against the princes of earthly power,‡ Michael's deeper battle is with Satan and his minion forces of darkness. The intent of the serpent and his angels is to bring humans to death apart from God. But the comforting news is that Christ has defeated the foes and Michael has been at Christ's side doing battle.

Comfort about the future in the face of death

Nothing is more fearful to humans than the future that awaits us just beyond the veil of this life. Before I tell a story about divine comfort as we face that kind of future, let's look at an event in the life of the apostle Paul. He took a journey from Jerusalem and Caesarea to Rome across the broad-backed Mediterranean with its mysterious waves and sudden storms and reputed sea monsters lurking below the surface. The sea journey began innocently enough, but the ship encountered a ripping storm. It is not unfair to describe this as a cosmic battle:§

> When a gentle south wind began to blow, they saw their opportunity; so they weighed anchor and sailed along the shore of Crete. Before very long, a wind of hurricane force, called the Northeaster, swept down from the island.

---

* Colossians 1:15–20; 2:15
† Revelation 12:7–9
‡ Daniel 10:13, 21
§ Acts 27

The ship's captain decided not to fight the storm but to let it take them where it wanted. For three days they were driven by fierce winds and eventually had to throw nearly everything into the sea. Most had given up hope. Food was running out, death was staring the sea stragglers in the face, and then Paul got a visit from a surprising stranger. (Was it Michael?) The angel arrived with comforting news, and here's what Paul told the boat's frightened occupants.

> Last night an angel of the God to whom I belong and whom I serve stood
> beside me and said, "Do not be afraid, Paul. You must stand trial before
> Caesar; and God has graciously given you the lives of all who sail with you."
> So keep up your courage, men, for I have faith in God that it will happen just
> as he told me. Nevertheless, we must run aground on some island.

Paul found comfort in this: you will survive and will be tried in Caesar's courts. For Paul and the others on the boat, the comfort was that they would survive. When you are neck-deep in the waves of the Mediterranean, when food is dwindling, and when the future looks like a funeral cavern in the depths of the sea, the promise of survival is good news of comfort.

As we walk forward into darkness or at best into dim grayness in life, God sometimes sends an angel to comfort us and to give us courage to take the next step. In Marilyn Chandler McEntyre's memoir-like record of ministry in hospices, she gives us this reminder while a loved one was lying on a deathbed of angelic, divine comfort:

> Last night, someone was in the room with me. People are in and out all the
> time these days, even at nighttime, but this was different. I felt witnessed,
> accompanied, held, and blessed by a presence I couldn't name. I don't really
> need to give it a name, though I believe in angels, and in the special ways the
> Spirit may show up, and that Jesus is with us always and God is omnipresent.
> All these are matters of belief. The visitor who came last night infused those
> beliefs with an immediacy and an intimacy that felt both natural and
> mysterious.

It's hard to speak of such things, even to the people I love and trust. These days, drugs can be mind-altering and neurological signals confused. This was a sacred moment I don't want to submit to analysis or kindly condescension or clinical dismissiveness. It filled me, and fills me still, with peace and gratitude. It brought a sense of light, though not light visible to the eye, and stirred the air so subtly I would hardly call it movement, but something more like a shift in ambient energy.

I think I am being met and reassured: I won't have to travel this passage alone. I am not alone. Love bids me welcome. . . .

I have every confidence that I am being and will be cared for both by earthly and heavenly helpers. Perhaps I have been all along.[3]

She was hearing the hum of angels as divine comfort.

ANGELS AS GOD'S VERY PRESENCE

One of the first riddles about angels in the Bible is the question of who is "the angel of YHWH" or "the angel of the LORD." We encounter this angel frequently in the Old Testament.* There are too many instances to quote in full here, but the Bible citations for the verses that follow can be found in the footnote at the bottom of the page. Here are a few typical examples (please read them carefully):

> The angel of the LORD found Hagar near a spring in the desert; it was the spring that is beside the road to Shur. And he said, "Hagar, slave of Sarai, where have you come from, and where are you going?"

> God heard the boy crying, and the angel of God called to Hagar from heaven and said to her, "What is the matter, Hagar? Do not be afraid; God has heard the boy crying as he lies there. Lift the boy up and take him by the hand, for I will make him into a great nation."

> There the angel of the LORD appeared to him in flames of fire from within a bush. Moses saw that though the bush was on fire it did not burn up.

---

* Genesis 16:7–12 [7-8 quoted]; 21:17–18 [quoted]; 22:11–18; Exodus 3:2 [quoted]; Judges 2:1–4; 5:23; 6:11–24 [11-12 quoted]; 13:3–22 [v. 3 quoted]; 2 Samuel 24:16; Zechariah 1:12 [1:12 quoted]; 3:1; 12:8

The angel of the LORD came and sat down under the oak in Ophrah that belonged to Joash the Abiezrite, where his son Gideon was threshing wheat in a winepress to keep it from the Midianites. When the angel of the LORD appeared to Gideon, he said, "The LORD is with you, mighty warrior."

The angel of the LORD appeared to her and said, "You are barren and childless, but you are going to become pregnant and give birth to a son."

Then the angel of the LORD said, "LORD Almighty, how long will you withhold mercy from Jerusalem and from the towns of Judah, which you have been angry with these seventy years?"

Who is this angel of the LORD? Is it the same angel each time? Most especially, might the Angel of the LORD be a *pre-Incarnation* appearance of Jesus on earth in the form of an angel? We call such pre-Incarnation appearances of Jesus "Christophanies." Or is this an appearance of God, thus a "theophany"? (We have noted previously several scenes from the Bible that show angels being confused with God.) So who is the Angel of the LORD? Just a regular (if there is such a thing) angel, a theophany, or a Christophany?

THE ANGEL OF THE LORD, JESUS, AND GOD

When Joshua learned that the man who appeared to him was the Angel of the LORD, he "fell facedown to the ground in reverence." The angel does not say, "Don't do that. Worship only God." But at the far end of the Bible, in the last chapter of Revelation, John falls down in front of an angel, and the angel explicitly rebukes him for doing so.* So at least in the case of Joshua 5:14, we know the angel is a manifestation of God.

At times the Angel of the LORD appears as a human, as when the three visitors appeared to Abraham. In that account, Abraham was "standing before the LORD."†

---

* Revelation 22:8–9
† Genesis 18

The wording does not qualify the reference by adding "the Angel of." When Jacob wrestled with God, he seemed to have been wrestling with a man. However, the wrestler is called God *and* an angel. The wrestler might or might not have been a pre-Incarnation visit to earth by Jesus.* And when Samson's parents encountered the Angel of the Lord, they thought it was both a man and God himself.† Jesus perhaps? Perhaps.

So inasmuch as the Angel of the Lord appears to be a human, that angel could perhaps be the Son of God who does eventually become human. But one thing surely disproves that Jesus appeared in the form of an angel-like human in the Old Testament. The same thing disproves that manifestations of the Angel of the Lord are Christophanies: no one in the New Testament suggested that Jesus of the New Testament was the Angel of the Lord of the Old Testament. Consider how many texts, figures, and images of the Old Testament are understood to have been fulfilled in Christ. Now consider that among these, not one suggests that he was the Angel of the Lord. We are left to conclude that the Angel of the Lord was not a Christophany.

There is yet another, even more convincing, reason not to think of the Angel of the Lord as a Christophany. The angel of the Lord *appears in the New Testament.* The appearances begin with Joseph in Matthew, and then move to Luke's Gospel, where we see a special appearance to the priest Zechariah:‡

> But after he had considered this, an angel of the Lord appeared to him in a dream.

> When Joseph woke up, he did what the angel of the Lord had commanded him.

> Then an angel of the Lord appeared to him [Zechariah, father of John the Baptist], standing at the right side of the altar of incense.

---

* Genesis 32; Hosea 12:4–5
† Judges 13
‡ Matthew 1:20, 24; Luke 1:11

The angel that appeared to Zechariah told him his name, which is Gabriel. If his name is Gabriel, he is not the Lord Jesus. There are then very solid reasons for not seeing the Angel of the LORD of the Old or New Testaments as referring to Jesus. They are instead manifestations of God's divine council sending an angel to serve us.

It is wiser to see Christ being present *wherever God is present,* but only because Christ is God, not because Christ was making a special pre-Incarnation appearance. What we do know is that *God becomes present* to humans in the Old Testament in a variety of ways, sometimes as an angel, and these angels communicate his loving care for their redemption.

In fact, this is so clear in the case of the Angel of the LORD it warrants a point-by-point listing:[1]

- The Angel of the LORD is identified as God.
- The Angel of the LORD is recognized as God.
- The Angel of the LORD is described in terms suitable to a reference to God.
- The Angel of the LORD calls himself God.
- The Angel of the LORD receives worship.
- The Angel of the LORD speaks with divine authority.

The conclusion is obvious: God becomes present with us in special ways in the Angel of the LORD. He does so to communicate his *presence,* his *love* for us, and his special concern for our *redemption.*

So the download for us is this: when an angel speaks, it is God speaking; when an angel acts, it is God acting; when an angel comforts, it is God comforting. The angels are sent by God to represent God. Which means whenever we hear the hum of an angel, we hear God; how we respond to the angel's hum is how we respond to God.

GOD'S EXPRESSIONS OF LOVING PRESENCE

God is love and all that God does is loving. Hence, sending angels from the divine council room is an act of love on God's part. Love, as we have seen, involves four elements: a rugged commitment to a person, a commitment to be present with another person, a commitment of presence that leads to the conviction that the loving person is our advocate and for us, and finally all of this love has a direction. Divine love leads to redemptive Christlikeness. We have looked at the first two elements—the rugged commitment in the form of God's covenant to Abraham and Sarah, as well as at God's commitment to be present with us. It is time now to turn to God's loving advocacy and see how the angels communicate that *God is for us*. Here again is the core teaching in the Bible about angels:

> God is Love.
>> All that God does is loving.
>> God sends angels to us because God loves us.
>> Love is a rugged commitment to be *With*,
>> to be *For* us so that we can
>> progress *Unto* Christlikeness.
>
>> Angels are sent to express God's love
>> by being God's presence with us, especially in the Angel
>>> of the LORD,
>> by being God's presence for us, and
>> to lead us into the redemption of Christlikeness.

Part 3

God's Loving Advocacy from Angels

GUIDANCE ANGELS

The enemy's design is to reduce life to the material, including erasing angels from our world. C. S. Lewis looked at this problem in his widely read *The Screwtape Letters,* an imaginary set of letters from one of Satan's underworkers, Screwtape, to his servant, Wormwood, about how to destroy the faith of a new Christian. Here is Screwtape's opening salvo:

> Thanks to processes which we set at work in them centuries ago, they
> find it all but impossible to believe in the unfamiliar while the familiar is
> before their eyes. Keep pressing home on him the *ordinariness* of things.

The process involves turning a person's gaze away from God and angels (the "unfamiliar") and toward themselves and the world (the "familiar"), what Lewis calls "contented worldliness." The spell cast over the world since the Enlightenment makes us all partakers of contented worldliness. Screwtape informs Wormwood that the two of them live in ambiguity about what to do:

> We are really faced with a cruel dilemma. When the humans disbelieve in
> our existence we lose all the pleasing results of direct terrorism and we make
> no magicians. On the other hand, when they believe in us, we cannot make
> them materialists and sceptics.

Screwtape has one design: "To us a human is primarily food; our aim is absorption of its will into ours, the increase of our own area of selfhood at its expense."[1] These lords of darkness don't want humans to disbelieve or to believe, they just want the humans' souls.

The strategy of our enemy is to turn our gaze from God and from his Son and his Spirit to ourselves and to our world. But opening our hearts to God and to the World Beyond is God's design. We turn now to the next line in the Bible's core teaching about angels, the line that reminds us that God sends angels to be with us because God and the angels are *for* us:

> God is Love.
> > All that God does is loving.
> > God sends angels to us because God loves us.
> > Love is a rugged commitment to be *With*,
> > to be *For* us so that we can
> > progress *Unto* Christlikeness.
>
> > Angels are sent to express God's love
> > by being God's presence with us,
> > *by being God's presence for us,* and
> > to lead us into the redemption of Christlikeness.

GUIDANCE INTO THE FUTURE

One of my favorite books is Charles Dickens's *A Christmas Carol,* a story that begins on a note of profound miserliness compounded by total disregard of the poverty of a young worker, Bob Cratchit. The miserly employer, Mr. Ebenezer Scrooge, meets his match when an angel-like ghost takes him on a journey through his life. They go back into his past, which leads deeper and deeper into his heart. They examine his wounds and miserly character. Scrooge is led to see that his own potential future depends on what path he will choose. Young children are spooked by the ghosts of

A Christmas Carol, while older folks need to be reminded that a journey-with-angels motif is found in the Bible and its world. The motif also is seen in Dante's *The Divine Comedy* and John Bunyan's *The Pilgrim's Progress.*[2]

The most famous biblical journey is found in the book of Revelation. Let's start where John starts in the first verse of the first chapter:

> The revelation from Jesus Christ, which God gave him to show his servants what must soon take place. He made it known by sending his angel to his servant John.

The entire book of Revelation is a revelation from Jesus Christ mediated to John *through an angel.* So entranced are we in theological speculations about Vladimir Putin or Bashar al-Assad or Benjamin Netanyahu (the most recent major figures to appear in such speculations) that we may forget that the book of Revelation is a journey into the future at the hand of God's revealing angel. Instead of speculating, we are to let the angel's hand guide us to see one grand vision after another. Eventually, the revelation will guide us to the New Jerusalem in the new heavens and the new earth. There, God's people will dwell in safety. Justice, peace, and love will flourish forever.

No one needs the guidance of this kind of angel more than modern Westerners trapped in a world designed by the enemy, that world being the realm of contented worldliness. We need to accompany John to benefit from the guidance of the revealing angel.

We see Jesus in all his glory in the middle of chapter 1, followed by a satellite view of seven churches in Asia Minor that reveal the good, the bad, and the ugly of the church. And each of the churches somehow summons us to be faithful.

The angel lifts us to heaven to see that no matter what life seems like on earth and no matter how oblivious we are to earth's being loaded with angels, God is on the throne. Nearby are the four living creatures (angelic beings of some sort) and the Lamb, who alone is worthy to open the scroll. The contents of the scroll will reveal what's in the next room and the room inside that room and the room just round the corner. There also are openings of books and seals plus multitudes of the redeemed praising God with the angels. And that's not all. There are trumpets and graphic scenes of judgment against those who inflict injustice in the world and much more. All of this comes to a head in two moves. We see that Babylon (surely Rome and all the empires Rome represents) is thoroughly defeated and the final city of justice then descends to earth.

In the future, we are shown, bad will lose and good will win. Speculations need to be laid aside if we want to grasp what John provides for us in the book of Revelation. It is not a blueprint with precise details of the future, but a travel guide to big themes.

Amid all that is going on in Revelation, angels are *guiding John* into the future where *redemption is found*. It's easy to see why we need this guidance. When we read the news, when we get absorbed in election campaigns that point to an earthly future that may turn against our deepest desires for a nation we love, when we face doom in a doctor's diagnosis—in all these settings we need that angel to take us to a point where we can see the world from God's perspective.

Angels always have guided God's people, including (at times) to a person to marry!

GUIDING US IN LOVE

Abraham is an old man and his incredible wife, Sarah, recently died. Isaac has reached the age where a marriage is not out of the question. Abraham gets his right-hand man to promise that he will see to it that (1) Isaac not only does not marry a Canaanite but instead joins his life to a woman from the home country and (2) they all return to the holy land God has given them. The servant goes to the home country but has his work cut out for him. It is not easy to be a stranger who suddenly shows up in a faraway place and seems to expect that a father will consent to give him his daughter. The servant is seeking a bride for Isaac, a man who didn't even come on the trip. And the unseen groom is the son of Abram, a man who deserted this faraway place years earlier. This is not a recipe for success.

But Abraham, who has seen God's redemption up close and beyond personal, knows something: God "will send *his angel* before you so that you can get a wife for my son from there."* The servant heads off for northwest Mesopotamia with ten camels loaded with goods designed to entice a father into surrendering his daughter in marriage. And guess what? It all works out.

The male leaders—Bethuel and Laban—are amazed by the providential circumstances of how the servant found Rebekah. They say, "This is from the LORD." Though they'd prefer Rebekah stay a little longer, they ask if she wants to go back with the servant to marry Isaac. She says, "I will go." All of this was engineered by an angel.

Today, Too

I recently experienced angelic guidance. I was asked to speak at a church in Florida, and my first response—besides being honored to be invited to speak—was *Why would this church, with a pastor I've never met, invite me to speak?* Even after agreeing to speak, I had my hesitations. But Kris and I, because we were in Florida during my sabbatical from Northern Seminary, drove to First Baptist Church in Tallahassee. An angel intervened between the two Sunday services.

In the pastor's office William Shiell, the pastor, asked me about Northern Seminary. I said we might, in the next year or so, be looking for a new president. Without having ever thought the thought or considered the statement, and *through angelic guidance,* I then said to William, "We need a president like you."

Then I felt that odd discomfort: *Why in the world did I say that?* William gave me a slight grin and shook his head in a kind of "thanks for that," but it went no further. (William later pointed out that what I had said was spoken in front of the church's executive pastor, who also was in the office.)

Six months or so later, I was part of a search committee tasked with identifying candidates to serve as the seminary's next president. Even though William's name had not been on my list of candidates, in a committee meeting I said, "William

---

* Genesis 24:7, 10 50, 58

Shiell." I had not given thought to William as a candidate until that (second angelic-inspired) moment. I cannot explain this apart from God's sending angels to whisper into our minds the plans of God for us.

Guess who was invited to be president of Northern Seminary? Guess who is now the president of Northern Seminary? William Shiell.

I believe the Bible is our sure way to know God's will, and that means I have always believed in angels—though I am very suspicious of the angels on Hallmark greeting cards and the chubby cherubs of Christian art. But as I researched and wrote *The Hum of Angels,* a gradual conviction arose within me: angels are far more present than we think. Here is why I am convinced of this. God loves us and that means God is with us. He is with us in a number of ways: as Father and as Son and as Spirit. But angels? Yes, and angels. Here's why: wherever God is at work, God's angels are both attending God in worship and *sent on mission* to accomplish specific tasks. As I write this sentence, the angels surround me. As you read this book, angels surround you. How do we know this? By faith and probably not by sight. But why by faith? Because the Bible teaches that God's angels surround the presence of God. Wherever God is, angels are present.

But angels are not cute doll-like beings, nor are they wispy see-through phantoms. The angels of the Bible, if we pay attention, often are fierce. Kathleen Norris, ever alert for our cultural superficialities, put it this way:

> The angels of scripture have an admirable self-possession. "Fear not" is
> what they always urge of the humans they encounter. But the angels
> populating the card, gift, and hobby shops of American malls suggest that
> there is nothing at all to fear. People who profess no belief in God will tell
> you that they believe in "personal angels," yet another sign that our secular
> society is anything but. Collecting angels in the form of figurines, mobiles,
> and dolls has become big business. New Age bookstores offer workshops on
> "angel channeling." What were once God's angels have become our own,
> fulfilling roles that other people might have taken, as confidant, friend, or
> therapist.[3]

But We Have to Listen and Obey

Sometimes an angel comes our way, and whether we acknowledge the angel or not, we ignore what God is prompting us to do. Here is a story from Jenny:

I never really thought much about angels and their influence on my life until a couple years ago. I've been sick for the past three-and-a-half years, and it all started the day on which I now know there were angels interceding and I chose not to listen or acknowledge them or she/he.

For a day in February I made an appointment to have a cosmetic procedure done at my dermatologist's office. I was a little leery about it, but at thirty-two and facing old age, I really was excited at the thought of holding back time a little with this procedure. [Jenny uses smilies here: ;).] I made the appointment for 4:30 and had scheduled a sitter, who called me at 4:15 to tell me she was in traffic and would be late. *No worries,* I thought! I'll call the doctor and let him know. Four thirty rolls around and the sitter calls to tell me her tire went flat! Five thirty rolls around, and she calls to tell me she fixed her tire and is on her way.

She doesn't show until 6:30. So I called the doctor to reschedule, and he told me to still come on in, he was working late and would still take me. I didn't get there until 7:30 because of other roadblocks that delayed me. . . .

Long story short, I had injections of Botox and ended up in the hospital with botulism and suffered horrifically for a full year and have been struggling to regain my health ever since!

Yes, we all feel the same way about this story: this is definitely a first-world problem. But I'd like you to notice what Jenny has learned from this experience, which included one delay after another. That series of delays are what she now thinks of as an angelic intervention that she chose to ignore:

I truly, wholeheartedly feel angels were at work to intervene and I chose not to listen. I try not to kick myself every day, but I don't make decisions lightly now.

GUIDING US TO WHAT GOD WANTS FOR US

Surely among the top three angel events in the Bible is the Angel of YHWH that guided the children of Israel from Egypt across the Red Sea and then through the wilderness into the Promised Land (Israel).* The Angel of YHWH leads God's people to what God most wants. If you read Exodus 23:20–33, you can see five of God's wants for Israel, with the Bible verse quoted first:

See, I am sending an angel ahead of you to guard you along the way and to
bring you to the place I have prepared.

(1) God wants to guard his people as they journey to God's place for them. In the same way that Jesus promised his disciples he would leave to go and prepare a place for them, so YHWH had a place—the Holy Land—prepared for his people. God promised they would get there under his guard. Similar language is used at times in the New Testament for God's guarding us until we get to the new heavens and the new earth.

Pay attention to him and listen to what he says. Do not rebel against him; he
will not forgive your rebellion, since my Name is in him.

(2) God wants his people to listen to the angel's wisdom. We are not told how much the angel talked, but we do know that in Exodus the Angel of YHWH and YHWH himself are so connected that their identities easily can be confused by the listener. In the words I just quoted from Exodus, the "him" is God speaking through the angel.

If you listen carefully to what he [the angel] says and do all that I [the angel's
words are God's words for Israel] say, I will be an enemy to your enemies and
will oppose those who oppose you.

---

* Exodus 23:20–33; 32:34. Especially also consider Exodus 3:1–10.

(3) God wants his people to know that he's got the angel's back. Notice how committed God is to the Angel of the LORD. The angel is so much the personal presence of God that we are exhorted to hear the angel's words as God's own words. Therefore, we are called to stick with the angel!

> I will establish your borders from the Red Sea to the Mediterranean Sea, and from the desert to the Euphrates River.

(4) God wants us to be victorious by following the wisdom of the angel. Victory for the children of Israel means living in a land of their own, which every nation needs and deserves. Victory means faithful worship of the one true God. Victory means abundance in resources and produce and health and a full house and a long life. Victory means respect and honor from other countries. These are promised by God to the faithful Israelites.

> Now an angel of the Lord [Yes, that angel and the same terms] said to Philip, "Go south to the road—the desert road—that goes down from Jerusalem to Gaza."

(5) God wants us to know that God's angel is still at work. Those who know the Bible's great theme about the Angel of YHWH hear an echo of that very same angel when they read about Philip the evangelist (above).* That surprising visit of the angel of the Lord led Philip to preach the gospel to the Ethiopian eunuch. In doing so, Philip pointed that man to the death of Jesus as the meaning of the suffering servant in Isaiah 53. This led to the expansion of the people of God into Africa.

God's angel guides the people to what God wants, and what God wants most is for the world to glorify him. We may not see the angel of the Lord at work today as Philip perhaps did, or we may not hear the voice of the angel of the Lord as he did, but this much is clear: the same God rules, the same God wants the same great things for all the world, and the angels of that same God are still at work to guide us to all that God wants for us. God so loves us that he sends angels our way to guide us.

---

* Acts 8:26–40

13

ADVOCATE ANGELS

We need to pause to bring all this together. The world is bigger than we think, for it abounds with God's creatures, including angels. God sometimes sends angels to us because God loves us. Since love means God's rugged commitment to be with us and for us so we will become Christlike, the presence of angels demonstrates God's love for us.

The presence of angels is not designed to convince us that there is more to this world than others think. Nor are they present so we can feel superior to others or be wowed by God's awesome power. And neither are they present so we can have great stories to tell. No, angels are sent on mission as our *advocates* for our *redemption*. We must emphasize this theme.

Love, we repeat, is God's rugged commitment to be present with us, to be for us as our advocate, with the goal of transforming us through redemption into Christlikeness. Angels are God's agents of redemption, and one of the Bible's great, but largely neglected, examples of this comes from the prophet Zechariah. Because what follows is not known to many churchgoers, I want to dwell on Zechariah's angel-and-redemption story.

GOOD NEWS TO THE FIRST ZECHARIAH

A good way to think about Zechariah is to imagine yourself as a young child deeply in love with your community. Your community was that of your great-grandparents and your grandparents and your parents and your uncles and aunts and their ancestors. The kind of community where you know everyone and everyone knows you, where every building and field generates a story from some old codger spurred by a never-to-be-forgotten memory.

Then imagine a stranger comes along and takes you to a foreign land where people speak a different language and eat different foods and worship different gods. They also resort to brutal violence against others when they think it's necessary. Imagine you've been in that foreign land far too long. You realize you have settled into these routines and have learned new stories. But no matter how settled you are, you refuse to accept a sense of belonging in this place. Your hope and dream is to return home before you die.

That was the world of one of the Old Testament's greatest prophets, Zechariah. His people Israel (or Judah) were living in captivity in Babylon. They had been there far too long, and they wanted to return home. But for some reason, their covenant God had only recently stirred to action to put an end to their exile. God created a new kind of exodus and pulled off a return home for his people. The prophet had been waiting along with everyone else, and he had a habit of asking the religious leaders, "How long?" The people had been longing for a prophet who would tell them some good news.

Now, back to some imagining. The good news came, and you packed your belongings and rounded up all the members of your family who had survived the exile in Babylon. You returned to the land of Israel, the land God promised to Abraham. You're back now, you're old, and there's not much time left, but still you're back. But the old stories you have heard about Jerusalem don't match the Jerusalem you now see. You ache and hope (like a Cubs fan) to see Jerusalem return to its former glory. (The angel part is coming soon.)

The Samaritan people, opponents of the Jews, are threatened by the new empowerment program in Jerusalem. They do everything they can to block the reestablishment of Jerusalem. You are glad to be back in the land, but you long for peace and a return to the golden days. Those days will not return until (1) the enemy powers and oppressors end their occupation and enslavement of the people of God, (2) God returns in glory to the temple and begins to rule the people again,

(3) the people begin to live as God wants, and (4) God blesses the people as in the old days.

The *foundational relationship* of God to Israel is this: I will be your God and you will be my people. That relationship is embodied in God's glorious presence in the temple, both guarded and announced by the cherubim. God's presence, then, is the sign of reconciliation; God's absence is the sign of a people who have chosen to ignore God. So it's all about God's presence in the temple. Zechariah is all over this heart-of-hearts vision. Now we come to the angel.

Most people who read Zechariah start to finish—as it is meant to be read—come away confused. Some even say the writing is jumbled. We don't have space here for a long investigation, so I will draw our attention to the angels' communications with Zechariah and how they reveal good news for people of hope. The angels on mission gave Zechariah five prophetic messages to deliver to God's people, and these sermons were designed to fire their imaginations to see the potential of what God would work.

First, the good news is that God loved them and was on their side. Zechariah's message begins with an astounding revelation: we are the "apple of [God's] eye."* Love means jealousy, which is the fire experienced in the belly of the lover who knows love has been spurned. So the angel tells Zechariah that God says, "I am very jealous for Jerusalem and Zion," and then later says, "I am burning with jealousy for her."† God wants Israel to love God—every person in Israel, from the most common peasant to the highest priest.

Second, God is ready to act. One of the more powerful images in all of the prophetic literature can be seen when Zechariah says:

> "Shout and be glad, Daughter Zion. For I am coming, and I will live among you," declares the LORD. ‡

Yes, of course, but the question is *How soon?* Here is the arresting image: YHWH is about to get up from the throne and unleash justice against injustice in the world.

---

* Zechariah 2:8
† Zechariah 1:14; 8:2
‡ Zechariah 2:10

Be still before the Lord, all mankind, because he has roused himself from his holy dwelling.*

Which now provokes a question about what God will do when he returns to Zion to dwell among the people.

Third, God will undo the injustices of the oppressors. Israel's prophets always had two themes: God will discipline Israel for sins, and God will rescue Israel from its sin-driven exile. The discipline, however, often is brought by foreigners who oppress the people and commit grave injustices. At one point in his prophecies, Zechariah said four craftsmen would defeat the oppressing rulers. At another point he said Satan was behind the evil injustice committed by those rulers. At yet another point, he said four chariots would go forth to defeat evil rulers.† The angel's message is clear: God will defeat injustice to bring Israel back to Jerusalem. The exile is over. (*Woohoo*, you say.)

What will happen then? Fourth, God will reconcile the people to God and to one another. The signs of revival will appear when unspiritual priests will be forgiven and restored, when the faithful return to Jerusalem to rebuild the temple, cities, and walls, and when the people obey God. The angel passed on great promises through Zechariah. Israel would once again flourish in the land. Notice the angel-sent messages of good news:

> "Proclaim further: This is what the Lord Almighty says: 'My towns will again overflow with prosperity, and the Lord will again comfort Zion and choose Jerusalem.'" . . .
>
> "'In that day each of you will invite your neighbor to sit under your vine and fig tree,' declares the Lord Almighty." . . .
>
> This is what the Lord Almighty says: "Once again men and women of ripe old age will sit in the streets of Jerusalem, each of them with cane in hand because of their age. The city streets will be filled with boys and girls playing there." . . .

---

* Zechariah 2:13
† Zechariah 1:18–20; 3:1–2; 6:1–8

And the Lord Almighty will shield them.
They will destroy
and overcome with slingstones.
They will drink and roar as with wine;
they will be full like a bowl
used for sprinkling the corners of the altar.
The Lord their God will save his people on that day
as a shepherd saves his flock.
They will sparkle in his land
like jewels in a crown.
How attractive and beautiful they will be!
Grain will make the young men thrive,
and new wine the young women. *

We New Testament believers too often ignore the truth that God's redemption, the very reason angels are sent as our advocates, is more than spiritual salvation. God's salvation, from the beginning of the Bible to the end in the New Jerusalem, is a whole people having a holistic redemption. This is personal, familial, communal, and national. It is thriving in a new city and a new land and in a new heaven and a new earth. Zechariah announced this long ago and—back to the imagination—you get to hear him announce it.

Fifth, God will permanently dwell with his people in a new king. God announced that he will return, and when he returns many nations (catch this, because this is a surprise in the prophecy) will worship the Lord God of Israel.

"For I am coming, and I will live among you," declares the Lord. "Many
nations will be joined with the Lord in that day and will become my people.
I will live among you and you will know that the Lord Almighty has sent me
to you."†

---

* Zechariah 1:17; 3:10; 8:4–5; 9:15–17
† Zechariah 2:10–11

Gentiles will become "my people"? *When? How? How soon?* And these are just the questions that come immediately to mind. Now watch what happens:

> Rejoice greatly, Daughter Zion!
>> Shout, Daughter Jerusalem!
> See, your king comes to you,
>> righteous and victorious,
> lowly and riding on a donkey,
>> on a colt, the foal of a donkey.*

In this wonderful, angel-delivered message to Zechariah, we see an obscure figure called the Branch, surely an image for the coming Messiah.† Those very words, you may well recognize, were used for Jesus when he entered the temple on a donkey on the last week.‡ In Zechariah's prophecy, when the Branch comes, what will happen? Justice will happen for the whole world and peace, the Messiah's peace, will rule!

> I will take away the chariots from Ephraim
>> and the warhorses from Jerusalem,
>> and the battle bow will be broken.
> He will proclaim peace to the nations.
>> His rule will extend from sea to sea
>> and from the River to the ends of the earth.§

All through this long explanation, we see nothing less than an angel's revelations from God to Zechariah for a people floundering but on the edge of flourishing. These prophecies will fire their imaginations to work for what God alone can create, and these prophecies are a clear message from God. It is now known that God loves Israel, God is for Israel, and God will redeem Israel. But keep in mind that

---

* Zechariah 9:9
† Zechariah 3:8; 6:12
‡ Matthew 21:1–11, especially verse 5.
§ Zechariah 9:10

redemption here is not limited to "getting saved." Redemption is whole-nation-whole-body redemption.

AGNATHA EXPERIENCED ANGEL-PROMPTED REDEMPTION

Sometimes we are tempted to think that God did these things for ancient Israel, but no longer does God intervene in this way. Don't tell Agnatha (not her real name) that because she knows angels are still in the business of communicating God's redemption to us.[1]

It was a warm and sunshine-filled morning. It was one of those June mornings that we take for granted in the Midwest. I was driving to my job, my head filled with not much of anything. I had started this job less than two months earlier after being unemployed for more than nine months. It was a great job, but one that paid only a little more than half the salary I had been making previously. I felt God call me to this job and knew somehow He would provide.

As I drove I noticed smoke coming through the car's air vents and I thought something was wrong with the air conditioner. I tried to put the window down but it wouldn't budge. Then I noticed flames shooting out from under the hood. In a moment flames were shooting in through the dashboard. I tried to pull the car over, but as I applied the brakes, I realized I had none. The road I was driving on rolled gently up and down for at least a mile. I panicked, not knowing what to do. The car filled with smoke, and I could no longer see what was ahead of me. I threw the car into park but it kept rolling. I turned off the ignition but the car continued to roll. My eyes burned from the smoke, and I began to be lightheaded.

The car finally came to a stop. I tried to find the door handle but I was disoriented from the thick black smoke. My legs began to burn now that the flames were lapping at them. I still couldn't find the door handle. I cried out, "Jesus, help me!"

Suddenly, the door opened, and a woman dressed completely in white held out her hand. She led me to the median. I hugged her and thanked her for rescuing me. Just then the car blew up, sending debris into the air. She hugged me, sheltering me with her body. I thought to myself, "How am I going to afford a new car?" With that the woman took my face in her hands. She looked at me with the kindest eyes I had ever seen and said, "Agnatha, I promise you everything will be okay." As she removed her hands from my face, I noticed my purse on the ground. I didn't remember having grabbed it. I turned to thank the woman for getting my purse, but she was gone.

A policeman arrived and I asked if he had seen my rescuer. He assured me no one was with me when he arrived. I began to cry as I realized God had sent an angel to lead me safely from the fire.

Redemption in the Bible is not just spiritual, it is holistic. Agnatha experienced the redemption of God at the hands of an angel sent on mission.

GOOD NEWS TO THE SECOND ZECHARIAH AND ELIZABETH

Angels are spirits sent by God to humans so they will know what God is about to do. Zechariah promised the return of God to the temple in both the figure of the Branch and in the image of a king riding into Jerusalem on the most inglorious of animals, a donkey. Once the New Testament sets the record straight, we learn that the Branch is Jesus, the donkey rider is Jesus, and the donkey's ingloriousness symbolizes the cross—the oddest way in history for God to assume his rule over the world. In those inglorious oddities, however, the gospel becomes clear: God enters into our death so that we might live eternally in the New Jerusalem, in the new heavens and new earth, where God will be with us once and forever.

We learn almost all of this through angels. Which is why the angel Gabriel seems so prominent in the earliest announcements that the Branch was here, the donkey rider had arrived, and his name was Jesus. Gabriel starts building a throne for the Messiah by revealing to two old folks, Zechariah (not the prophet) and Elizabeth, that they will have a baby named John, who, in angel-like fashion, will be sent to announce the arrival of the Messiah. But Gabriel begins by telling some Abraham-and-Sarah-like good news of family creation:

The angel said to [Zechariah], "I am Gabriel. I stand in the presence of God, and I have been sent to speak to you and to tell you this good news."

The well-beyond-the-age-for-giving-birth Elizabeth's response? (Surely you detect here a subtle comment about Zechariah's own capacities.)

"The Lord has done this for me," she said. "In these days he has shown his favor and taken away my disgrace among the people."

Gabriel has accomplished his mission with Zechariah and Elizabeth, so he moves on to Mary:

"Greetings, you who are highly favored! The Lord is with you."

Angels don't appear for nothing, so Gabriel's first move is both effective—it got Mary's attention—and ambiguous. She must have been thinking, *There's got to be more to this story, because angels don't just show up to say hello.*

Mary was greatly troubled at his words and wondered what kind of greeting this might be. But the angel said to her, "Do not be afraid, Mary; you have found favor with God. You will conceive and give birth to a son, and you are to call him Jesus. He will be great and will be called the Son of the Most High. The Lord God will give him the throne of his father David, and he will reign over Jacob's descendants forever; his kingdom will never end."*

These words add detail to Gabriel's "highly favored" with "Son of the Most High." That is, Mary's favored mission is to be mother to the Messiah, the Branch mentioned by the first Zechariah. There could have been no better news for a poor teenage woman who knew poverty, whose homeland experienced occupation by Rome. Mary, tradition tells us, was from Sepphoris, just an hour's walk north from Nazareth.

---

* Luke 1:19, 25, 28–33

To be told her baby boy would be Messiah was a way of saying, *Farewell, Herod!* It was also a way of saying, *God's promise to Abraham and to our fathers is now being fulfilled.* And it was a way of saying that God's glorious *and holistic* redemption was about to be unleashed in the land. With these reasons, and no doubt more, jostling about in her excited heart and head, Mary highballs it to her relative Elizabeth. She wants the two of them to enjoy God's faithfulness together. When Mary gets to Elizabeth's she utters this song, one of the Bible's greatest songs of redemption. This is exactly the kind of redemption news that began when Gabriel was sent by God to inform these holy families of what was about to happen in Israel and the world.

Mary said:

My soul glorifies the Lord
  and my spirit rejoices in God my Savior,
for he has been mindful
  of the humble state of his servant.
From now on all generations will call me blessed,
    for the Mighty One has done great things for me—
    holy is his name.
His mercy extends to those who fear him,
    from generation to generation.
He has performed mighty deeds with his arm;
    he has scattered those who are proud in their inmost thoughts.
He has brought down rulers from their thrones
    but has lifted up the humble.
He has filled the hungry with good things
    but has sent the rich away empty.
He has helped his servant Israel,
    remembering to be merciful
to Abraham and his descendants forever,
    just as he promised our ancestors.*

---

* Luke 1:46–55

One more time to bring this all into focus: God loves us, and God's love means presence and advocacy so we can become Christlike. To foster that redemptive Christlikeness, God sends angels to guide us toward redemption. No clearer guide to the redemptive ministry of angels can be found than tying together the first Zechariah with the second Zechariah, who is the relative of Zechariah's messianic Branch, King Jesus. King Jesus brings the fullness of redemption.

14

GUARDIAN ANGELS

The most common belief about angels is that we have guardian angels. When it comes to guardian angels, the Roman Catholic tradition finds no competitors. The Feast of the Holy Guardian Angels is celebrated every year on October 2. Official Catholic teachings are contained in *The Catechism of the Catholic Church*, and this is what we read:

> [A summary belief in guardian angels comes first.] From its beginning until death, human life is surrounded by their watchful care and intercession. [Then a quotation from a church father, Basil:] "Beside each believer stands an angel as protector and shepherd leading him to life." [Another summary statement completes the section.] Already here on earth the Christian life shares by faith in the blessed company of angels and men united in God.[1]

In a footnote in the *Catechism,* Bible references are given for the opening statement of belief in guardian angels, including the texts we will consider in this chapter. But what the Bible says is the big issue because some Protestant theologians have reacted strongly against every assertion made in the Roman Catholic catechism. Does every believer or person in the world indeed have a guardian angel or not?

Back to the *Catechism.* The history of guardian-angel theology in the Roman Catholic Church unfolds into a myriad of ideas and distinctions. When that long and intricate history is held against the three sentences in the *Catechism* quote above, it reveals how Spartan the *Catechism* is. For all that history, the *Catechism* has chosen to reduce it to basics. But Roman Catholicism is not alone in affirming guardian angels. Valery Rees has summed up the story of world religions in these words: "The idea that there are angelic beings appointed to guide and guard the way we progress through life is common to so many traditions that it is hard to escape the conclusion that we are dealing with an archetypal mode of human experience."[2]

Others know their guardian angel by name or by voice. Peter Kreeft, a philosopher, dedicated his book on angels to "Francis and Frodo, my wife's and my guardian angels." Martin Israel, a scientist by training no less, confesses this:

> I know my angel, surely my guardian angel in whom I believe absolutely, by his insistent voice in my life. Whenever I have done anything clearly wrong in my relationship with someone else, my angel has made me aware of my misdemeanor in no uncertain way. His insistence that I put matters right, and as soon as possible, cannot be evaded. The things I have done wrong have not been major offences, but instead the tendency to be irritable and impatient with someone who was clearly seeking my assistance. On one occasion much earlier in my life. . . . [And off he goes on stories and teachings, including thanking God daily for the angel's help in guidance and instruction.][3]

Some are inclined to believe in guardian angels because it is part of their church's teachings. Others believe in them because so many different religions affirm them. And others are believers due to having had profound experiences with their guardian angel. But what does the Bible teach about guardian angels? Are we too comfortable in our "contented worldliness," to use those words of C. S. Lewis again, to consider guardian angels?

THE BALANCE BEAM

Once again we are led to the balance beam. If we deny angels as guardians, we deny the Bible; if we accept guardian angels, we may well join the many who have gone way too far; if we ignore them altogether, we may be missing once again the hum of angels. Someone who walked this balance beam with eyes-wide-open faith is the great reformer, Martin Luther:

> It happens to many a man that he will escape fire, water, murder, and other misfortunes because of some insignificant thing that has moved him. Such a thought, or whatever it may be, comes to him so that he does, all at once, the thing that saves him, a thing which he could never have foreseen or thought beforehand but of which he must say, "Indeed, if I had done this or that, I surely should have drowned, been burned to death or murdered, or died or suffered harm in some other way"; or, as someone else might say, "You had your guardian angel with you there." The Gentiles therefore ascribed such happenings to good fortune and made an idol of fortune. For they saw and learned that such things happened but did not know that the true God had done them through His holy angels.[4]

The opposite of skepticism about angels is no-holds-barred belief, which can be illustrated by Bellarmine, a Roman Catholic who, in his famous book on how the mind ascends the ladder to God, spoke of guardian angels accompanying all important people and offices:

> There are two kings, one a man and visible, the other an angel and invisible; and in each church there are two bishops, one a man and visible, the other an angel and invisible; and in the universal Catholic Church there are two supreme pontiffs established under Christ the Lord, one a man and visible, and one an angel and invisible, who we believe is the Archangel Michael.[5]

Bellarmine, a Jesuit, represents a typical Catholic view, as does the so-called *Angele Dei,* the prayer to one's guardian angel: "Angel of God, to whom I am confided for celestial happiness, illuminate me today, guard me, direct me, govern me."[6] Slipping off the balance beam? At times, for sure. In fact, historian Trevor Johnson turns a critical eye toward this sort of imbalance by concluding that at times, guardian-angel piety becomes a "substitute pneumatology."[7] That is, what God does through his Spirit is sometimes shoved over to the credit of angels.

Two of the most influential theologians in the history of the church, Basil the Great and John Chrysostom, taught that every Christian has a *personal* guardian angel. Most theologians have agreed, most pastors have trusted the theologians, and most Christians in pews have accepted such teaching.

COLD WATER ON THE TRADITION

Until John Calvin, that is. Those who have followed in the wake of Calvin have tended to minimize guardian angels. After sketching the many instances in the Bible where God commissioned angels to protect and help the people of God, Calvin emptied buckets of cold water on the tradition of each person's having a guardian angel. "But whether individual angels have been assigned to individual believers for their protection, I dare not affirm with confidence." One might then ask if Calvin too had fallen off the Bible's balance beam. His response relieves the tension: "We ought to hold as fact that the care of each one of us is not the task of one angel only, but all with one consent watch over our salvation."[8]

Instead of believing in helicopter angels, Calvin believed God was watching and protecting, and that God *sometimes* sent an angel to watch or protect his people. No less, no more. Not one angel per person but divine protection. In the history of the church, no one was more fiercely biblical in commitment than John Calvin. For that reason alone he deserves our ear.

But one has to wonder if his solution to an exaggerated allegiance to the per-capita assignment of guardian angels in church tradition is not reverse exaggeration. The solution is faith in the Bible's balance beam. Calvin was pushing against exaggerations by exaggerating in the other direction, and his exaggeration was needed to restore the balance. But after thinking through some of the discussion-stopping criticisms of Calvin, American author Joel Miller steadies himself on the beam with these words: "If we had the free eyes of faith, we would see ourselves standing side by side with winged guides and guardians."[9] A biblical faith must be open to the hum of guardian angels, so we repeat the core Bible teaching about angels:

God is Love.
>All that God does is loving.
>God sends angels to us because God loves us.
>Love is a rugged commitment to be *With*,
>to be *For* us so that we can
>progress *Unto* Christlikeness.

>Angels are sent to express God's love
>by being God's presence with us,
>*by being God's presence for us in guarding us,* and
>to lead us into the redemption of Christlikeness.

THE BIBLE AND GUARDIAN ANGELS

It is too easy to jump to Jesus's famous statement and then, like Jack Horner who poked his thumb into the Christmas pie to find a plum and proclaimed himself a good little boy, announce to the world that one believes in guardian angels. Before we can stick our thumb into Jesus's pie of angels, we need to back way up in the story of God in the Bible. If it is too easy to grab Bible references—out of context and for our advantage—from Jesus, it also is too easy to forget the lines above: God loves us and *that is where we must begin.* We will never understand guardian angels unless we begin with God's love. If God loves us, and if love means God is present with us, and if God sends angels our way, then it is entirely consistent with God's love to send guardians to be present with us. The whole Bible must be comprehended to understand guardian angels, not just a verse or two.

The three formative events in the Old Testament are the *Creation,* the *covenant* God made with Abram, and the *Exodus* from Egypt. Creation occurred before we were awake, and the covenant occurred with Abram asleep. The *Exodus* event was comparatively chaotic and violent and the stuff of movies. The battle was on between Moses and Pharaoh, and it took far more than an army of chubby cherubs or trumpet-blowing seraphs to triumph over the "horse and his rider." But the children of Israel did triumph, and from that victory until they reached the homeland, Israel was in need of, well, nothing less than a *mega–guardian angel*. The kind of guardian angel that could guide them from Egypt through the desert to the land of Israel. As God explicitly said, "See, I am sending an angel ahead of you to guard you along the way and to bring you to the place I have prepared."* The mega–guardian angel for the children of Israel was the Angel of Yhwh, whom we discussed in an earlier chapter.

Once again, Yhwh and the Angel of Yhwh are barely distinguishable. Was it God, was it an angel, was it Jesus prior to his incarnation? We need to remind ourselves that the hum of an angel is the hum of God. Read the two paragraphs that follow, and see that what is said of Yhwh in the first description is said of the Angel of Yhwh in the second.†

First, a description of Yhwh.

By day the LORD went ahead of them in a pillar of cloud to guide them on
their way and by night in a pillar of fire to give them light, so that they could
travel by day or night. Neither the pillar of cloud by day nor the pillar of fire
by night left its place in front of the people.

Now, a description of the Angel of Yhwh.

Then the angel of God, who had been traveling in front of Israel's army,
withdrew and went behind them. The pillar of cloud also moved from in
front and stood behind them, coming between the armies of Egypt and
Israel. Throughout the night the cloud brought darkness to the one side
and light to the other side; so neither went near the other all night long.

This is the beginning of the guardian-angel theme in the Bible. It is one angel, not hundreds of thousands, and it is more about *God guarding his people* than each person having an angel. But this is only the beginning of the theme.

Angels guarding us is found in a number of places in the Bible, and we should

---

* Exodus 23:20
† Exodus 13:21–22; 14:19–20

do better than ignore such clear statements.* First, *Jacob* (who also is called Israel) says an angel has been guarding him:

> "The Angel who has delivered me from all harm
>   —may he bless these boys.
> May they be called by my name
>   and the names of my fathers Abraham and Isaac,
> and may they increase greatly
>   on the earth."

We hear a similar idea from David in two different psalms:

> The angel of the LORD encamps around those who fear him,
>   and he delivers them.
> For he will command his angels concerning you
>   to guard you in all your ways.

It doesn't stop there. In prison, Daniel is visited by the archangel Michael, who was sent on mission by God to help Daniel. The help offered by Michael was by way of comfort and to reveal to Daniel what was happening. This type of assistance is not limited to the big boys of the Old Testament. It also is found in crucial moments in the New Testament. Acts 12 includes a famous story about Peter being guarded by an angel. And Paul was guarded by an angel at the time of a shipwreck on the Mediterranean Sea. The writer of Hebrews at least suggested that angels are sent to guard and protect us in our journey toward final redemption.

JESUS AND GUARDIAN ANGELS

Now it is time to stick our thumbs into the Jesus pie. Undoubtedly, the most secure text in the Bible for supporting belief in a guardian angel can be found in a word of Jesus:

---

* The following discussion cites verses from Genesis 48:16; Psalm 34:7; 91:11; Daniel 10:13–21; Acts 12:15; 27:23–24; Matthew 18:10; and Hebrews 1:14.

See that you do not despise one of these little ones. For I tell you that *their angels in heaven* always see the face of my Father in heaven.*

We can debate with the rest of the theologians in the history of the church who the "little ones" are (Christians only, children of Christians, all babies, all humans). We also can debate when the guardian angels are sent (at conception, at birth, at baptism, at conversion). But it is more than a little difficult to deny Jesus his point. He sticks the word "their" on the forehead of the little ones and on the forehead of the angels in heaven and draws a straight line between them.

Much speculation, as I say, has sparked much conversation in the church regarding how God assigns guardian angels and whether a guardian angel is tailored to fit us or one is paired to complement us. We can debate until we're out of breath, but *we don't know.* Let us learn to let the Bible be the Bible and the Bible's teachings about angels be the Bible's teachings about angels. We need nothing more, and much of the debate that originates outside the words of Scripture is either not needed or is nothing more than speculation. While much of the speculation is little more than grist for an interesting discussion, it also can be dangerous. Consider, for example, the belief that our guardian angel sits atop one shoulder and a wicked angel, again assigned to us, on the other.

What we do know is that God loves us, that God's angels care about us, and that God sends angels *to protect and guard us.* Does each of us have a lifelong guardian angel? Perhaps. What matters more is that God loves us and however God chooses to accomplish redemption, he has sent angels our way to guard us.

TWO STORIES

I don't base my belief in guardian angels on stories of someone's being protected by an angel or even because I've had such experiences. Rather, the Bible affirms the reality of God guarding us in multiple ways by sending angels. But hearing others' stories can lift our faith.

---

* Matthew 18:10

This story comes from Charles Jaekle, author of a fine book on angels and the recorder of some fascinating angel experiences. He tells of a seventy-year-old retired fighter pilot in the US Air Force who, some fifty years earlier, had just completed a course in aerial acrobatics. Jaekle's words now:

> He was a self-assured, even cocky young man, he said, and when he set out to fly alone at night to Jacksonville, Florida, 190 miles away, he was sure he had set his altimeter to sound an alarm when his aircraft flew below 3,500 feet; he had, in fact, mistakenly set it at 200 feet.

It doesn't take much imagination to see where this story is headed: straight into a crash and the pilot's death. At 2 a.m. and just a few miles out from Jacksonville, this is what happened:

> He felt frisky enough to attempt a celebration by doing a figure eight, believing that he was well above 3,500 feet since his alarm had not sounded; when it did sound, he was confident he had sufficient altitude to complete his maneuver and level off. He rolled back his canopy as he leveled out, when he heard a voice telling him to look off his right wing. The voice spoke a second time and immediately afterward again, this time in a commanding, masculine voice. He obeyed the command, looked, and was horrified to see, just three feet beneath him, the furrows of a newly plowed field. Sure he was about to crash into that field, he began to scream. What flashed into his mind in that fraction of a second was the thought that his death would be very quick and his mother needn't worry because it wouldn't hurt. At that instant, he said, a powerful force—as if from outside himself—invaded his body so that he was able to respond with a superhuman effort. He pulled back on his controls and calculated that he had cleared the trees on the edge of the field by no more than six inches.[10]

A masculine voice, some superhuman power, a life-changing experience, and the pilot became a dedicated Christian.

From the children of Israel to Jesus and to the apostles, the Bible steadily records the presence of angels who are guarding us. So there are guardian angels sent on mission to keep us on mission. Do we each have a guardian angel? Jonathan Macy, after his careful study of angels in the Bible and in the history of the English church, has this to offer: "I would not be surprised if, when we get to glory, we find we have one [guardian angel] with a whole host of stories about how they were invisibly enriching our lives by their work."[11] Perhaps so, but for sure the Bible gives us confidence that God loves us and the angels care about us and are commissioned to guard us.

Angels are sent on mission as our advocates, but there is a great direction for all the work of angels. They are sent *from* a God of love to assist us in our journey *toward* redemption. Because redemption is the aim of God's love and the angels' mission, the angels always, always, always lead us to Jesus. This theme is so dense in the Bible I will devote the next three chapters to it.

ANNOUNCEMENT ANGELS

Here is the Bible's big message about angels. They are spirits sent on mission by God *to communicate divine truths* to us in order to keep us on mission in our journey toward redemption. Following the initial shock humans experience at an angel's appearance, the angel always divulges some divine secret. Which leads us to what is most important about what angels communicate:

> If the mission of an angel is to communicate divine truths to humans
>> and if the deepest truth of God is redemption in Jesus,
>> then it follows that angels will communicate *divine truths about Jesus.*

When you hear the hum of angels, you hear music about Jesus as King.

Stephen Noll's exceptional study of angels in the Bible includes this story of an apparent angel that keeps Christians on mission:

> Among my own acquaintance is a couple whose whole life plan was suddenly changed by an event that they identified as angelic intervention. Having just finished training for the Peace Corps, they testified at church one night about their hopes and plans. As they greeted folks after the service, a man they did not know came up and said, "But can you speak about Jesus [in the Peace

Corps]?" He then walked out of the building. Moments later they went after him to ask further what he meant. But he was gone. That night as they talked and prayed, they realized God was calling them to give up the Peace Corps and go into missionary service.[1]

This is not a story critical of the good done by the Peace Corps, nor is it a claim that everyone should do the missionary work of church planting instead of humanitarian work. No, this is a story about an angel doing what angels are sent on mission to do: *communicate divine truths about redemption in Jesus.* It's all found in the question the man asked: "But can you speak about Jesus?" What God wants the world to know about is Jesus.

This is demonstrated in the words of the angel Gabriel who appeared to Mary.

MARY, ANGELS, AND JESUS

Protestants tend to be comfortable with Mary only during Christmas season. But anyone who reads the Gospel of Luke carefully knows that God showers his favor on Mary in such a way that we are to see her as someone specially blessed by God. To Mary, the angel Gabriel revealed *all the important names, titles, and ministries of Jesus.* She was the first to know both who Jesus was and what he would accomplish. Here is Gabriel's encounter with Mary, including the words of the angel that reveal Jesus are rendered in italics:

> In the sixth month of Elizabeth's pregnancy, God sent the angel Gabriel to Nazareth, a town in Galilee, to a virgin pledged to be married to a man named Joseph, a descendant of David. The virgin's name was Mary. The angel went to her and said, "Greetings, you who are highly favored! The Lord is with you."
>
> Mary was greatly troubled at his words and wondered what kind of greeting this might be. But the angel said to her, "Do not be afraid, Mary; you have found favor with God. You will conceive and give birth to a *son,* and you are to call him *Jesus.* He will be *great* and will be called the *Son of the Most*

*High. The Lord God will give him the throne of his father David, and he
will reign over Jacob's descendants forever; his kingdom will never end."*

"How will this be," Mary asked the angel, "since I am a virgin?"

The angel answered, "The Holy Spirit will come on you, and the power
of the Most High will overshadow you. *So the holy one to be born will be
called the Son of God.* Even Elizabeth your relative is going to have a child in
her old age, and she who was said to be unable to conceive is in her sixth
month. For no word from God will ever fail."

"I am the Lord's servant," Mary answered. "May your word to me be
fulfilled." Then the angel left her.*

Gabriel made clear to Mary that her life's mission was to be "highly favored"
because the "Lord is with you" in a very special way. The fruit of her womb would
rule the world as God's Son, Israel's Messiah, and Lord. We might miss something
here: the angel's words revolutionized Mary's life, which became nothing less than a
Jesus-shaped life. I have traipsed through many, many churches in Europe, and I
have to confess that at times it's too much Mary and not enough Jesus. (That's not a
Protestant bias so much as a theological observation.) If you read again the exchange
between Mary and Gabriel from Luke 1, you will see what I'm saying. The conversation is not anywhere near as much about Mary as it is about Jesus. The angel's mission was to inform Mary not just about her role in God's mission but most especially
about the role of Jesus.

What is the role of Jesus? This can be answered by looking at three titles or la-
bels that Gabriel revealed about Jesus. The more we listen to the hum of angels the
more we will be led to Jesus.

ANGELS LEAD US TO JESUS AS KING

Gabriel's central statement about Jesus is this: Jesus "will be *great*" and Jesus will be
called "the Son of the Most High." Jesus will occupy "the throne of his father David"

---

* Luke 1:26–38

and Jesus "will reign over Jacob's descendants forever"; "His kingdom will never end." One word captures everything Gabriel revealed: *Messiah*.

What does this term mean? Israel is the people of God; God is the King over Israel; God permitted humans such as Saul and David and Josiah to rule his people for him, and the results were at best mixed. But God promised someday he would establish his own kind of King, the Messiah. When the Messiah came, God would re-establish his rule over his people Israel. God promised that when that happened the whole world would start joining the people of God, and this people (Gentiles included) is called the church. Jesus would be the one true Lord over this new people of God.

So when Mary heard these words from Gabriel, her response must have combined responses such as "It's about time!" and "Finally!" In Mary's time, this reaction would have come out like "Hallelujah!" It also combined expressions such as "Get rid of Roman rule!" and "Let us now dwell in peace and salvation and joy and faithfulness!" and "Justice for the poor!" and "Food for the hungry!" and, most especially "God's kingdom has arrived!" Along with this chaser: "This will last forever and ever!"

All this and more for one reason only: Gabriel led Mary to see that God had sent his Son, King Jesus, the Messiah, to redeem and save and rescue the people from sin and injustice and slavery. If you hear the hum of angels you will hear music about Jesus as King.

ANGELS LEAD US TO JESUS AS LORD

Every Christmas we read (preferably in the King James Version) the wonderful narrative from Luke's second chapter, beginning with the majestic and very Roman-sounding "And it came to pass in those days, that there went out a decree from Caesar Augustus, that all the world should be taxed. (And this taxing was first made when Cyrenius was governor of Syria.) And all went to be taxed, every one into his own city."* Joseph and the very pregnant Mary traveled to Bethlehem, where she gave birth to Jesus.

---

* Luke 2:1–3, KJV

We find three scenes in the second chapter of Luke's Gospel: Caesar Augustus ruling the Roman empire from a throne of godlike power in Rome; the altogether lowly Mary and Joseph and the baby who had to be placed in an animal's manger because lodging space in Bethlehem was occupied to capacity; and some night-dreaming shepherds in a field visited by angels. Consider that out of this cast of the earthly great (Caesar) and the earthly blessed with the imminent arrival of a son (Mary and Joseph), it was to the shepherds out in a field to whom the Angel of the Lord appeared. Why? To reveal what was happening nearby.

"Do not be afraid. I bring you good news that will cause great joy for all the people. Today in the town of David a Savior has been born to you; he is the Messiah, *the Lord*. This will be a sign to you: You will find a baby wrapped in cloths and lying in a manger."*

Note the angel's use of *the Lord*. Remember the three scenes: Imperial Rome, the manger, and the shepherds. The angel told the shepherds that the baby was the Lord, and that title meant Caesar was no longer lord of the realm. *Jesus was now Lord*. Once again we have angels sent on mission to communicate divine truths. The focus is not on Augustus or Joseph and Mary or the manger itself or on the supposed lack of hospitality shown to the young couple arriving on a donkey. Nor is it on shepherds or angels. The focus here is on who the baby in the manger is, and one word stands out: he is the Lord.

One more observation: the angel was suddenly accompanied by "a great company of the heavenly host . . . praising God and saying, 'Glory to God in the highest heaven, and on earth peace to those on whom his favor rests.'"† One angel became a multitude of angels.

The Bible doesn't clarify who they were, but some theologians have suggested that these were the angels who are appointed to guard each nation and tribe in the world.[2] That is, "great company" was the collection of the guardians of the whole world gathered around the world's true King, Jesus, to announce

---

* Luke 2:10–12
† Luke 2: 13–14

the world's peace through Jesus. I don't know if that interpretation is accurate, but I know the message is true: for this baby in the manger, the whole world bends in worship. He is Lord of the Realm.

If anyone were to listen to the angels, they would hear a song about the cosmic lordship of Jesus. Caesar, too, will have to bow before this Lord. Martin Israel, in his book about angels, has observed that the "judgement on such sources [and so-called revelations from angels] should always be: do these communications lead the hearer to a more Christ-like frame of mind . . . or [are] they merely messages of complacency leading to self-satisfaction?"[3] His question is neither asked frequently enough nor answered often enough.

ANGELS LEAD US TO JESUS AS SAVIOR

Now we need to look at the third title for Jesus in the Gospel accounts of the birth of Jesus. In Matthew's Gospel* the same "angel of the Lord" appears. The angel informs the Torah-observant Joseph that his fiancée is pregnant outside the normal method for getting pregnant, and this gets Joseph's Torah-wheels aspinnin' with surprise and probably some anger and decisions to divorce her so he can sustain his honor and be obedient. But the angel tells him the out-of-the-ordinary circumstances are all in God's plan, which Joseph no doubt has some doubts about. The amazing moment in the account is that Joseph chooses to go along with the plan.

The angel tells Joseph what to call the son of Mary: *Jesus*. In Hebrew the name was *Yeshua,* and the angel interprets the name by saying, "he will save his people from their sins." Every time Jesus is called *Jesus,* he is being announced as Israel's *redeemer,* Israel's *rescuer,* Israel's *liberator,* Israel's *Savior. Jesus* was the name revealed to Mary when the angel first divulged that he would be the King[†] and when probably the same angel revealed to the shepherds the cosmic and empire-wide significance of the child in the manger.[‡]

The angel points each of these people to Jesus, and to each person the angel declares that this baby boy will grow to be the Savior. Salvation in the Bible is holis-

---

* Matthew 1:18–25
† Luke 1:31
‡ Luke 2:11

tic: Jesus will save God's people *politically* by giving them God's long-awaited Messiah King; he will save them *socially* by establishing a King who will bring justice, peace, and love; he will save them *physically* by healing them; he will save them *emotionally* by restoring them to themselves and to one another; and he will save them *spiritually* by wiping away their guilt and sins and transgressions.

The angels also are humming this same title today: Jesus is the *Savior*.

THE GOSPEL RULE FOR ANGELS

Here is a guiding rule in all experiences of angels: angels that do not lead us to Jesus as King, Lord, and Savior are not spirits on God's mission but false spirits. Angels in the Bible lead us to Jesus. Angel experiences that do not draw us to God's Son must be held either loosely or not at all. Angel experiences may well lead people to think there is more than meets the eye or that there is a "hum" of the divine all about us— but without taking us far enough. Frankly, the vast majority of angel experiences evoke transcendence at the most, but no element of leading a person to Jesus.

The angel experiences of the Bible anticipate the coming of Christ and then announce who Jesus is and what Jesus has accomplished.

Every time.

World without end.

Hallelujah!

16

TEMPTATION ANGELS

One of the Bible's great passages about angels is found in the first chapter of Hebrews. The text contrasts angels with Jesus.* For instance, angels are "spirits" and "flames of fire," but Jesus is the "Son" who has been set "above your companions." And it is the Son, not angels, who sits at the "right hand" of God.

This next set of lines says all that needs to be said: "When God brings his firstborn [Son] into the world" what does God announce? "Let all God's angels worship him." Angels may be powerful, supernatural beings; they may have special missions of communication; and they are more like fiery flashes of power than chubby cherubs. But angels are created to *worship* Jesus as God's Son and Lord. Jesus, the book of Hebrews continues, was made lower than the angels for a short spell of about thirty years in order to accomplish redemption, but then was exalted far above all angels and powers.†

Here we get a glimpse of the relationship between Jesus and angels. They worship Jesus, they are sent to lead humans to see the redemption Jesus has accomplished, and so they ultimately lead humans to join them in worship of Jesus.

This same glimpse can be found in the first chapter of John's Gospel. We read that Jesus summoned the early disciples into participating in his mission to announce eternal life and the kingdom of God. One of the disciples, Nathanael, expressed surprise that Jesus knew so much about him after Jesus revealed what

---

* I quote from Hebrews 1:5, 6, 7, 9, and 13.
† Hebrews 2:5–9

Nathanael had been doing when he was alone. Nathanael was awed by who Jesus is and so confessed him to be the "king of Israel."

Jesus then told Nathanael something about the heart of the mission of angels: "You will see heaven open, and the angels of God ascending and descending on the Son of Man."* This up-and-down movement of angels demonstrates the glorious centrality of Jesus in God's redemptive plan. Jesus, that plan announces, is the Lord of the Realm. Angels point the world to that Lord.

AT THE END OF THE TEST

God has set you on a journey, and you may wonder if you have what it takes to complete the journey. You may be tempted to cave in, but you know God has called you, that God is faithful, and that God will be with you. Jesus has been on that path before you, and if you listen for the hum of angels, you will hear them singing about Jesus. Jesus has walked our path before us, and the angels are opening up glimpses for us to see him ahead of us—sometimes waiting for us and other times pressing forward to challenge us to keep on.

Two or three paragraphs into the Gospel of Mark, we read that as soon as Jesus was baptized in the Jordan, the Spirit sent him out into the wilderness forty days.† Mark's Gospel tells us Jesus was "being tempted by Satan," but Matthew ramps the temptations up to the highest level with these words: "After fasting forty days and forty nights, he was hungry." (For sure.) The temptation came from the source of all temptations, Satan or the devil, and the temptation concerned food. Jesus was tested maximally in a physical manner.

Matthew continues the account. The devil took Jesus to the highest point in Jerusalem and, because Jesus knew he was God's Son—King, Lord, Savior—the evil one tempted him to jump off the pinnacle to prove he was God's special agent in this world. Jesus was tempted maximally at the level of trust and protection. Finally, the devil took him to a high mountain, showed him the cosmos that God had

---

* John 1:43–51, quoting 1:51. This passage sounds very much like the revelation of God to Jacob in Genesis 28:12–13.
† Mark 1:12; Matthew 4:1–11

promised he would rule, and told Jesus that he (Satan) would anoint him Lord of the Empire right now if Jesus would bow down to him (Satan) as to God. Satan tested Jesus maximally by offering Jesus everything God promised.

One more observation before we are surprised by some angels. At times we use the temptation narrative to learn how we can face temptation. First-century Jewish readers (not to ignore Jesus's own experience) would not have read the Bible that way, and in fact they would have thought it was idolatrous to see ourselves in that one-of-a-kind account. The story about Jesus's testing in the wilderness quotes three famous passages from the book of Deuteronomy, and they tell us not which verses to quote when we are tempted but about the Bible's deep narrative. Those passages detail Israel's years of demanding preparation before they were able to enter the Holy Land.*

We need to draw a line now from the Old to the New Testament. God tested Israel for forty *years,* and those forty years were compressed by God for Jesus into forty *days.* In forty days Jesus experienced what Israel experienced over forty years. Why? To prepare him to enter into the Land and conquer the Land so he could rule as the one true and faithful King over the people of God. So instead of thinking Jesus got off easy because he was in the wilderness for only forty days, we are to see instead that he was tested in the most severe manner. Now to the angels.

In Matthew's Gospel, Satan used the following words in the second temptation, misused for the sake of tempting Jesus: God "will command his angels" to protect Jesus. But Jesus refused Satan's offer because he knew God sends spirits on mission when God wants, not when humans demand them. But if we read this story carefully we will discover that the angels were not absent. Mark and Matthew both tell us that when the forty days of testing were completed, "angels came and attended him."†

One gets the impression that during the entire forty days, angels were watching as if they were the audience at some great thriller. The angels cared deeply about what was going on. But they were constrained by God until the moment the testing was done. Then God sent the spirits on mission to care for and provide solace for Jesus.

---

* The three passages Jesus quotes in Matthew 4:1–11 are from Deuteronomy 8:3; 6:16; and 6:13.
† Mark 1:13; Matthew 4:11

Immediately, the Son of God was in communion through the angels with his one and only eternal Father. Follow the angels and their concerns, and you will discover once again that they always lead us to Jesus. They show us that, though what God is doing in this world seems inscrutable, God is preparing this world for its one true and eternal King, King Jesus.

IN THE MIDST OF OUR TESTS

Angels are all around us even when we don't take notice of them. We are wise to believe they surround us, rather than expect them to announce themselves. What we learn from the Bible, though, is that they care deeply about what is going on with humans. One gets the impression they are always in their starting blocks, ready to dash off as soon as the starting gun sounds. But their appearance is rare enough for us to conclude they appear only when God thinks something special is needed.

We saw that the angels were held back from helping Jesus for forty days. A similar kind of sudden, surprising, but needed appearance can be found near the end of Jesus's public ministry. I will quote Luke:

Jesus went out as usual to the Mount of Olives, and his disciples followed him. On reaching the place, he said to them, "Pray that you will not fall into temptation." He withdrew about a stone's throw beyond them, knelt down and prayed, "Father, if you are willing, take this cup from me; yet not my will, but yours be done." *An angel from heaven appeared to him and strengthened him.* And being in anguish, he prayed more earnestly, and his sweat was like drops of blood falling to the ground.*

Let's back up to gain some appreciation for the moment. God had promised to rule the world in justice, peace, and love. But humans continued to refuse God's rule. God's promise to Israel was that they would be given the Messiah, who would

---

* Luke 22:39–44

rule the world through them. To Joseph and Mary, the angel Gabriel announced that those days have arrived and that their son, Jesus, would rule as King, Lord, and Savior. They were no doubt all for it, and the sooner the better.

What they did not know was how unusual the climb uphill to that throne would be. They had not realized that God's Messiah would enter into his rule after being tested and after suffering.

Jesus knew the suffering that awaited him. Like all who lived in the ancient Middle East, he knew the brutality of Rome and the utter fickleness of Pilate. He knew that saving their own skin would be far more attractive to the leaders than finding out who was truly innocent. He knew one of his closest friends, Judas, would be consumed by greed to the point of betraying Jesus to the Roman officials.

So in Gethsemane on the night of his betrayal, Jesus was in pain at all levels—emotional, psychological, and even physical. He was in such pain that he begged the Father to consider another way, but he willingly (and surely in utter faithfulness) submitted to God's plan. Jesus's suffering would end the grip of sin and sickness and selfishness on this world.

We are about to see that the angels strengthened Jesus. That would not have been needed if he had not been in a weak condition as a result of the stress of the test before him.

In the midst of Jesus's sweat-and-blood-inducing petitions before God, "an angel from heaven appeared to him and *strengthened* him." Not only before his birth and at his birth, but from the beginning of his ministry to the end of his ministry, angels were sent on mission to comfort Jesus as he reclaimed this world for God. The angels' first concern was Jesus, that he maintain his strength and take comfort in the presence and love of the Father. But let's remind ourselves again: Jesus could only have needed strengthening if the test had weakened him. He took a journey that is similar to ours, from weakness to strength.

We should see from this that God loves us, that God is our advocate, and that God sometimes sends angels to be our advocates by pointing us to Jesus. If the angels are advocates for Jesus by leading us to him, they are present with us to lead us to see Jesus's need of strengthening. Perhaps we can take comfort in Jesus's need for comfort as we too seek comfort from God in the deep stresses of our life's tests.

Here are the main lines of the Bible's teaching about angels once again, high-lighting in italics the emphasis of this chapter:

> God is Love.
>> All that God does is loving.
>> God sends angels to us because God loves us.
>> Love is a rugged commitment to be *With*,
>> to be *For* us so that we can
>> progress *Unto* Christlikeness.

> Angels are sent to express God's love
>> by being God's presence with us,
>> by being God's presence *for* us *in leading us to see Jesus as Lord*, and
>> to lead us into the redemption of Christlikeness.

BEFORE IT ALL BEGAN

I don't wonder if this is speculative. It has to be the case even if the Bible doesn't address it directly. Prior to his birth Jesus knew the joy of fellowship with the angels, and he also knew their adoration and worship. It is then worth observing that at his birth, Jesus was not for the first time experiencing angels. Neither did he find it unusual to encounter angels in the Garden of Gethsemane. As Jonathan Macy has stated so well:

> Angels are present throughout and around-about the life and ministry of
> Jesus, but you should remember that the plain Gospel accounts would not
> have been his only experience of them. Prior to the incarnation, Jesus, as the
> Second Person of the Trinity, would have had personal experience of angels
> both in heaven and on earth. As their Creator God, he would have known
> exactly what substance and nature they were; how they lived, acted, and
> thought, and how their society was ordered; he would have watched them fall

and then drag humanity down with them; and he would have been acutely aware of what he then had to do to put things right—the incarnation and the cross.[1]

Jesus and angels are together; to believe in Jesus is to believe in angels. The angels sent on mission are angels that, if we listen for their hum, will point us to Jesus. We will see in Jesus the one who has been through the test and endured it, and the one who came out of the test even stronger.

17

BIG-EVENT ANGELS

Angels care about humans so much that they peer over the edge of heaven to see what's happening on earth. But they care *far more* about Jesus. We can reverse the order to see the fuller truth. Because angels adore Jesus as the personal heart of God's mission, they care about humans participating in that mission.

Here's how we know of their superabundant care about Jesus. Angels surround the *big events* in the life of Jesus: the announcement of his birth, his birth, his forty days of intense testing, and his pain at Gethsemane. But the angels continue to focus our attention on Jesus in four more events that we will discuss here. Each of these events has altered history; each is epochal.

JESUS AND THE ANGELS

Even if Europe's famous art displayed in churches and museums depicts angels as Cupid-like babies or as wraith-like seraphs, that art has something profoundly biblical about it. The biblical aspect is that the angels usually are shown focusing on Jesus. We can turn the observation around: angels that don't lead us to Jesus are no longer on mission.

T. F. Torrance has told the story of his father, a missionary in China, and how an angel gave his father's gospel tract to a seeker:

One day he [Torrance's father] received a letter from a Chinese who had never heard of the gospel, but who recounted that all his life he had been seeking for eternal life, and had made long pilgrimages to various shrines and temples in pursuit of his quest. One night after many years he dreamed that in his travels along a mountain road he came to a great stone arch with the words chiseled on it "The Way to Eternal Life." As he made to go through the arch he was confronted by a man in white garments who asked what he wanted, and when he spoke of his search for eternal life, he was told to enter, but in his excitement he woke up. As soon as morning arrived he went to tell a friend about his dream, and on his way encountered a stranger in the village who thrust into his hand a piece of paper bearing the very words of his dream, "The Way to Eternal Life." It was a tract written by my father about Jesus as the Way, the Truth and the Life apart from whom there is no way to the Father (Jn 14:6). It had my father's name and address printed at the bottom. God had sent his angel to that Chinese pilgrim to show him the way to the Lord Jesus Christ, the one Mediator between God and humanity, whom to know and believe is to have eternal life.[1]

The point deserves emphasis because today, far too many angel stories have nothing to do with Jesus. They seem instead to be designed to enhance spirituality or to enhance one's experience. Angels in God's service are sent on mission to communicate divine truths about Jesus. Beware of angels that enhance a person's glory and avoid Jesus.

We learn more about the Jesus-centeredness of angels from their presence at four of the last events in Jesus's earthly life.

AT THE TOMB: DEATH IS DEFEATED, LIFE WINS

Our Christian faith opens up a whole new life, or it shuts it all down in this moment: the resurrection of Jesus on Easter Sunday. All four Gospels record encounters with time's magical first hours after Jesus's resurrection.* A recurring element in the Gos-

---

* Matthew 28:1–10; Mark 16:1–8; Luke 24:1–11; John 20:1–18

pel accounts is the presence of an angel, or two angels, or two men. These accounts illustrate once again a common pattern in the Bible: almost every time an angel appears, those who experience the angel confuse the angel with a human. One Gospel tells us the Angel of the Lord descended from heaven to the tomb and sat on the stone in a dazzling appearance. The angel rolled back the stone for the two women (both named Mary, by far the most common name for a woman in the first-century Jewish world), gave the women a brief tour of the tomb, explained that God had raised Jesus from the dead, and instructed them to tell the disciples. After all that, the angel revealed to the women that they would all see Jesus again in Galilee.

The other Gospels fill in other details. For instance, there were three women present (add Salome) and they saw one young man inside the tomb; another Gospel says the women saw two men in glistening clothing and the angels reminded the women that Jesus had predicted his resurrection. Each of the Gospels informs us that the women did as they were instructed and told the disciples, and that Peter and John ran to the tomb to see for themselves. John's Gospel also tells us of Mary Magdalene's encounter with Jesus. She wept because she feared someone had defiled the grave and stolen the body. Jesus appeared to her flanked by two dazzling angels, consoled her, and sent her off to inform the disciples.

The moment of realizing Jesus's body was not there and that he had been—of all things!—raised from the dead easily eclipses other details. Everything that matters most about the resurrection was conveyed first to the women by *angels*. Angels opened the tomb, they ushered the women into the tomb, they explained what had happened, and they issued next steps to take. What got overlooked in the excitement and wonder was that death had officially, physically, and ultimately been defeated. New creation was now afoot, and the last word would no longer be death but life.

CONFUSION ABOUT WHAT ANGELS LOOK LIKE

It's not hard to notice that those who came to the tomb were confused. Some of the witnesses thought one angel was present, others two, others thought it was two young men. So what was it? One or two angels? A man or two men? One hesitates to gain clarity for reading the Bible by appealing to modern appearances of angels.

But perhaps I can explain it like this: modern experiences of angels record a variety of physical experiences and various sights, sounds, and smells. If this is at all true, we may just have a little more sympathy for those who first encountered angels at the empty tomb.

After her extensive investigation into angel experiences, Emma Heathcote-James produced a pie chart showing what angels look like today. Perhaps this can help us understand what angels were like in the first century.[2] Almost one-third of witnesses saw a traditional angel figure in white. Others saw a human-like figure (17 percent); some experienced a scent of some sort (10 percent); while others encountered what seems nothing more than a bright light (13 percent).

The bright light is consistent with my only confident experience with an angel, if it was an angel, some forty-five years ago. I can recall it as if it took place this morning. Now back to the pie chart. Some witnesses had a physical sensation (9 percent); others an internal sensation (5 percent); and (11 percent) felt another visceral sensation. A small percentage encountered an angel through sound alone (5 percent).

I don't want to suggest that everyone who claims to have encountered an angel has done so. But what this broad spectrum of experiences reveals is the manifold modes of experience one might have in encountering at least a claim to an angel encounter. I can understand the confusion of those who came to the tomb better because of Heathcote-James's conclusions. Now on to another epochal event.

At the Ascension: Jesus Now Rules

Jesus didn't come to earth just to die for our sins; nor did Jesus come just to die and then be raised. We settle at times for too little. No, Jesus came to earth to live, to die, to be buried, to be raised, and then to ascend to the Father so he could rule as God's Son over all creation. At least forty days after the resurrection, Jesus was with his followers when he was lifted from earth into a cloud. We call this the Ascension. Jesus's ascension altered history forever. No longer did Caesar rule, and no longer did his proxy in the Holy Land rule. Jesus defeated the ultimate enemy, death, and cracked the bonds of death by rising from the realm of the dead. He not only defeated death but was exalted to the right hand of the Father and now and forever rules. Jesus is King regardless of what Caesar might think. The ascension of Jesus is a subversive message to all the empires of the world.

Perhaps by now we are not surprised by the presence of angels at the Ascension. Two angels were there, in fact, and they are described in a way that indicates they might well have been the same two angels (or was it two young men?) who appeared at the tomb.

> They were looking intently up into the sky as he was going, when suddenly two men dressed in white stood beside them. "Men of Galilee," they said, "why do you stand here looking into the sky? This same Jesus, who has been taken from you into heaven, will come back in the same way you have seen him go into heaven."*

The angels' mission was and remains to communicate divine truths about Jesus, and at the Ascension they were on hand to explain where Jesus was going.

The disciples would not know how to explain what happened had the angels not explained to them what the Ascension means. But there is more here: the angels wondered aloud why the disciples were standing there. Why were they not acting on what Jesus had just said about being witnesses? The angels' question was designed to remind the disciples of their mission to the world to tell others about Jesus. We repeat: angels are sent on mission to send us on mission and to keep us on mission.

Now, on to a third epochal, history-altering event.

AT JESUS'S RETURN: CREATION IS RESTORED

The New Testament gives witness to the presence of angels at the return of Christ. When Jesus comes back to reclaim his throne and usher the earth into the new heavens and the new earth, or to restore all creation to its divine condition, he will be surrounded by angels.† I will quote but one statement from Jesus and then one from the apostle Paul:

---

* Acts 1:10–11
† Mark 8:38; Matthew 25:31; 1 Thessalonians 4:15; 2 Thessalonians 1:7, 9

When the Son of Man comes in his glory, and all the angels with him, he
will sit on his glorious throne.

This will happen when the Lord Jesus is revealed from heaven in blazing
fire with his powerful angels.

Heaven, the apostle John has informed us in the book of Revelation, is a place
where Jesus is enthroned as the Lamb. The Lamb is surrounded by "thousands upon
thousands, and ten thousand times ten thousand" of angels. And they seem to do
nothing but sing praises to the glory of the Lamb.* So intense is that worship that
angels are sent to earth where they lead us in joining the angelic choir in praise to the
Lamb.

It is no wonder that when the Lamb returns to earth to redeem his people for the
kingdom of God, he will be surrounded like an emperor with a host of angels singing his praises. As they sing, they will focus humanity's attention on the King who
is victorious and who will rule forever. And then, as Jesus restores all creation, angels
will accompany him. Life in the new heavens and the new earth will never be the
same again. The angels surely will enjoy that great moment.

AT THE FINAL JUDGMENT: THE BOOKS ARE SETTLED

Heaven will not be heaven, nor will the present earth be able to be the new
heavens and the new earth, until all things are made right. We sometimes swal-
low up what the Bible teaches about the final heaven with our desire for personal
happiness and with our questions clamoring for answers. But the very essence of
heaven is this: God will make all things right, and heaven can't be heaven until
all things are made right. So this one, cosmically significant idea must be front
and center: evil must be defeated, judged, and destroyed forever. The threat of
evil, injustice, murder, violence, and abuse must come to its end in God's final
judgment.

More than a few times in Scripture, angels are depicted as *those who will execute*

---

* Revelation 5:11–12

the final judgment on God's behalf. Jesus told his disciples in parables that angels will be present at the judgment on behalf of Jesus:

> The field is the world, and the good seed stands for the people of the kingdom. The weeds are the people of the evil one, and the enemy who sows them is the devil. The harvest is the end of the age, and the harvesters are angels. . . .
>
> This is how it will be at the end of the age. The angels will come and separate the wicked from the righteous.*

God will judge and Jesus will judge, but this language reveals that angels are involved in the final judgment of separating the wicked from the righteous. Hence, angels are stationed at the gates, as it were, opening and shutting the doors.

When the judgment is over, when the books are finally settled, and once the angels have completed this final task, history's meaning will become fully clear. God's people will be praising God; they will abound in fellowship with one another in justice, peace, reconciliation, and love.

And know this: angels will be there, for they have been there all along, leading us to Jesus as the very meaning of history. "All things," the apostle Paul said, "have been created through him and for him."† The beginning of all creation is centered on Christ, and the goal of all creation is centered on Christ. Angels have no mission other than to lead us to the Lamb on the throne.

---

* Matthew 13:38–39, 49
† See Colossians 1:16.

WARRIOR ANGELS

The Bible reveals that not all angels are good. It depicts bad angels—demons, Satan, the principalities and powers—as constantly seeking to seize control of governments. What happens if bad angels begin to control bad humans? Care to name a few countries? Or cities? Or states? Or economic systems? Or educational strategies? Or laws of the land?

It is a sign of modernity that we hesitate to see the work of bad angels behind bad governments. A sign of the Bible is to see the work of bad angels behind bad governments.

THEY NOW WEAR MASKS

God created angels—immaterial beings, minds without bodies—and gave to them the charter for a life of eternal, God-serving freedom. Some angels followed the charter, some didn't. Because some didn't, there are bad angels and good angels, and good angels have the task of leading us into battle against bad angels. (This grossly simplifies a story that has more murky puddles than a trail through a rainforest, but this is not the place to sort out all the debates.) Adam and Eve sinned when they refused to listen to God and thought they could become like God. With their decision, Godlikeness was ruined and became Godlessness or God-unlikeness.

If that was the human sin, then what was the sin of angels? They committed the same sin: they disrespected God. They dishonored God and instead chose to honor themselves. They wanted autonomy. In the early church, another view of the precise sin of angels was this: angels sinned when some of them, myriads evidently, refused to acknowledge that humans were the ones chosen to be made in the image of God.[1] Their sin then was not the pride of autonomy, but rather the sin of envy. However we explain it, they sinned and became instruments of evil in God's good world. In an attempt to hide their evil intentions, they wear masks. As Paul observed, "Satan himself masquerades as an angel of light."[*] If this is true of Satan, it is certain for his diabolical servants, the evil spirits or demons.

THE BATTLE IN THE BIBLE

Here's a secret about the Bible: there is more adventure, more conflict, more battle, and more triumph than most readers seem to recognize. The Bible is the original script for *The Chronicles of Narnia, The Hobbit* and *The Lord of the Rings,* and *Harry Potter.* It is not at all mistaken to say the Bible displays God at war. If God is waging war against evil and the devil's minions, and we are on God's team, then we are summoned into the cosmic battle of life.

The book of Revelation, in the twelfth chapter, informs us that the battle is being waged and that the archangel Michael leads the good angels. Satan, of course, leads the dark angels, which puts Jesus in battle against the Antichrist and the dragon. The twelfth chapter lifts the veil to look into the heavenly, cosmic realms. It is there that we see the battle that has raged since the angels found autonomy and discovered they could deal destruction and death.

This is why one of the great prayers in the church asks God to send angels to be our advocates in the cosmic battle. It is a prayer that is prayed by Christians on Michaelmas, the day when we celebrate the archangel Michael, the archangels, and all the good angels.

O Everlasting God, who hast ordained and constituted the ministries of
angels and men in a wonderful order: Mercifully grant that, as thy holy angels

---

* 2 Corinthians 11:14

always serve and worship thee in heaven, so by thy appointment they may help and defend us on earth; through Jesus Christ our Lord, who liveth and reigneth with thee and the Holy Spirit, one God, for ever and ever. *Amen.*[2]

Before we enter further into the cosmic battle story found in the Bible, let's pause for an important announcement. The gospel is the good news that God's one true King, Jesus, defeated all the enemies at these epochal, history-altering events: at the Cross and at the Resurrection. That same Jesus has ascended to the throne of God where he rules. Those who enter into his rule by faith and allegiance to the world's one true King are guarded by the King, by the Spirit, and by God the Father. *Also,* and here is our theme for this chapter, we are guarded by the King's army of good angels.

THE OLD TESTAMENT "PRINCES" OF DARKNESS

It's easy to miss something when reading the following words from Moses recorded in Deuteronomy. So after we look at Moses's words I will examine them in light of a psalm. As you read these lines from Deuteronomy, notice the reference to "sons of Israel."

> When the Most High gave the nations their inheritance,
>   when he divided all mankind,
> he set up boundaries for the peoples
>   according to the number of *the sons of Israel.*
> For the LORD's portion is his people,
>   Jacob his allotted inheritance.[*]

What does "sons of Israel" mean? When this was translated into Greek centuries after the fact, the problem was resolved because "sons of Israel" became "sons of God." And "sons of God" meant "angels." Which is what we find in Psalm 82 and then later in Isaiah. Here are some of the more important lines:

---

* Deuteronomy 32:8–9

God presides in the great assembly;

> he renders judgment among the "gods" [= angels].

In that day the LORD will punish

> the powers in the heavens above
>
> and the kings on the earth below.*

In these passages we enter a story of a cosmos inhabited by angels who are as-signed to nations. And we are about to see that some of these angels are called *princes* (some of whom are good and some bad). An angel of revelation appeared to Daniel and described the details of a cosmic battle that was beyond human gaze. The battle is waged between angel-princes:

> But the [angel-]prince of the Persian kingdom resisted me twenty-one days. Then [the archangel] Michael, one of the chief princes [of the cosmic angels], came to help me, because I was detained there with the king of Persia. . . .
>
> So he said, "Do you know why I have come to you? Soon I will return to fight against the prince of Persia, and when I go, the prince of Greece will come; but first I will tell you what is written in the Book of Truth. (No one supports me against them except Michael, your prince.) . . .
>
> "At that time Michael, the great prince who protects your people, will arise. There will be a time of distress such as has not happened from the beginning of nations until then. But at that time your people—everyone whose name is found written in the book—will be delivered." †

We can put this all into one clear idea: the Old Testament world was inhabited by spirits, by angels both good and bad. In that world, which at times seems to be a worldwide assembly before God, God had assigned to each nation a "prince," an angel or archangel, but some of these angels chose the way of evil, injustice, oppres-sion, and idolatry. The contest between nations, then, is a contest between angels.

---

* Psalm 82:1; Isaiah 24:21
† Daniel 10:13, 20–21; 12:1

The Old Testament teaches that angels use nations to fight their battles! The archangel Michael seems to be one of Israel's special angels, leading Israel in a cosmic battle against evil and injustice.

The cosmic battle is a hum that can be heard every day on the Internet. All you need do to hear it is to read the news or follow a Twitter feed.

Some might want to dismiss the cosmic battle as archaic thinking. In the last month I have watched on video a Chicago police officer gun down a nonthreatening black man. I have read in the news media about other police officers who systemically covered up unjust violence committed against Chicago's most vulnerable. I have watched the news about a mass shooting carried out by radical Islamists in San Bernardino, California. Friends describe systemic injustices in countries such as Ukraine, Libya, South Africa, Pakistan, and the United States. We all have seen Americans demonize other Americans over political matters that in the grand scale of our global society are little more than petty differences. We are confronted with a question: is this how God wants us to live or are sinister forces at work?

Behind these scenes of evil in our world are sinister angels. Christians need to restore a belief in the world of bad angels at work in our world. Bad angels destroy, murder, and divide us. Notice these words that describe Chicago's corrupted law-enforcement system:

> Chicago police officers enforce a code of silence to protect one another when they shoot a citizen, giving some a sense they can do so with impunity.
>
> Their union protects them from rigorous scrutiny, enforcing a contract that can be an impediment to tough and timely investigations.
>
> The Independent Police Review Authority, the civilian agency meant to pierce that protection and investigate shootings of citizens by officers, is slow, overworked and, according to its many critics, biased in favor of the police.
>
> Prosecutors, meantime, almost never bring charges against officers in police shooting cases, seeming to show a lack of enthusiasm for arresting the people they depend on to make cases—even when video, an officer's history or other circumstances raise concerns.
>
> And the city of Chicago, which oversees that system, has a keen interest in

minimizing potential scandal; indeed, it has paid victims and their families millions of dollars to prevent information from becoming public when it fears the shooting details will roil neighborhoods and cause controversy for the mayor.[3]

Forget the politics—which is inherent to the problem!—and look at the impact. Humans could not have built a system this corrupt, this violent, this unfettered, and this destructive to people without outside help. The evil one lends a hand whenever the evil one can, and we see the evil outcomes all round us.

If our most recent news doesn't convince us of this, perhaps another source will. Jesus not only believed in the battle but entered the battle and came out the winner. His own battle with the principalities and powers reveals that the battle takes place in the heavenly realms as well as in the human heart.

Jesus Battles Evil Spirits

The disciples approached Jesus to say they had encountered a man exorcising demons, but that the exorcist was not one of Jesus's followers.[*] Jesus's response was *any kind of exorcism is a victory,* however small, even if associated with someone who was not in the inner circle. This account opens a big door on the world of Jesus, a world teeming with belief in angels and spirits. It is not surprising that Jesus battled evil forces by exorcising demons and evil spirits to liberate people to live for God.

In the Gospels, demons or evil spirits have but one aim—to destroy the life of the person.[†] That is, demons are out to capture individuals from *the inside out.* In the business of dealing death to others, demons perceive the mighty Jesus as a threat to their livelihood (better yet, their *death-lihood*), and they want Jesus to be gone. But Jesus confronts them with the power of God and exorcises demons by his mighty words. Then the person is set free to live for God. Demons, or the bad angels at work in this world, seek a foothold in a person's life in order to destroy that person.

Jesus once revealed how to understand his mighty acts of exorcism. "But if it is by the Spirit of God that I drive out demons, the kingdom of God has come upon

---

* Mark 9:38
† Here are four accounts: Mark 1:21–28; 5:1–20; 7:24–30; 9:14–29.

you."* Jesus's exorcisms were visible manifestations of God's saving, liberating power. Any reading of these accounts reveals a showdown between the forces of evil seeking destruction and death and the mighty force of life seeking redemption and life. The battle in the Bible takes place between God and evil, between Jesus and the demons, between the rule of God and the rule of the evil one.

Now we will learn that the angels are our advocates for life.

PAUL AND HIS ARMOR

The Bible's story has become clear: the cosmos is filled with spiritual beings. Some angels have been assigned to nations, and some of those nation-assigned angels have chosen the way of rebellion. But the bad angels can't be shoved off by assuming they are only at work in the world's principal cities of power. There are enough of them to work against every human on the planet. Life is a battle for you and me and not just for the nations. But at the head of the battle is the Lord of the good angels, Jesus the Lord, and his army of angels are sent as spirits on mission to lead us into the victory that he has himself accomplished.

How can we enter into this victory under King Jesus? The battle has been completed in the resurrection of Jesus but, because full redemption awaits the coming of heaven, that battle continues after the death, resurrection, ascension, and enthronement of Jesus. It continues not because the war's outcome is in jeopardy, but because God has a challenge for each of us: woman up or man up to the battle by arming yourself with spiritual armor. The apostle Paul's words deserve to be quoted in full:

Finally, be strong in the Lord and in his mighty power. Put on the full armor
of God, so that you can take your stand against the devil's schemes. For our
struggle is not against flesh and blood, but against the rulers, against the
authorities, against the powers of this dark world and against the spiritual
forces of evil in the heavenly realms. Therefore put on the full armor of God,
so that when the day of evil comes, you may be able to stand your ground,

---

* Matthew 12:28. Instead of "Spirit of God" the Gospel of Luke has "the finger of God" (Luke 11:20).

and after you have done everything, to stand. Stand firm then, with the belt of truth buckled around your waist, with the breastplate of righteousness in place, and with your feet fitted with the readiness that comes from the gospel of peace. In addition to all this, take up the shield of faith, with which you can extinguish all the flaming arrows of the evil one. Take the helmet of salvation and the sword of the Spirit, which is the word of God.*

We are engaged in a cosmic battle, which extends to the heart of each one of us. We are not fighting "flesh and blood," that is, external and material forms of life on earth. We battle instead "against the rulers . . . authorities . . . powers of this dark world and against the spiritual forces of evil in the heavenly realms." The systemic evil we experience in racism, classism, materialism, narcissism, or sensualism are not surface issues but expressions of the deeper spiritual war being waged. That war has but one aim: destruction to the point of death.

To wage this war our ascended and ruling Lord Jesus equips us with

- the belt of the truth that Jesus is Lord,
- the breastplate of righteousness or doing the will of God,
- the shoes that are prepared to take us into the world, offering the peace that our King brings,
- the shield of faith that protects us from the arrows of the evil spirits,
- the helmet of salvation that protects our heads, and
- the sword of the Spirit—the Word of God itself—that reveals the truth of the gospel and guards our every step.

We are in a battle. The war has been won by Jesus, but we are summoned to enter into his victory daily.

BRING THE BABIES FORWARD!

Baptisms of infants or baby dedications, either way, often are considered cute and charming and innocent and so very family-ish. Pictures a-snappin' and grandparents

---

* Ephesians 6:10–17

a-grinnin'—all the joy and celebration are part of it. Without diminishing the irresistible happiness associated with such events, I would like to draw our attention to the earliest records about baptisms. What has been said over babies in the history of the church makes some people today uncomfortable. A brief explanation now.

At the beginning of the third century, about AD 215, a leader in the Roman church named Hippolytus penned what we now call *The Apostolic Tradition*.[4] Before a person was to be baptized—a person of any age—the one to be baptized or the one speaking for the one to be baptized was to announce in front of all the church these words:

I renounce you, Satan, and all your service.

When this was done, "the presbyter [or elder] anoints him with the oil of exorcism that has been blessed, so that every evil spirit may depart from him."[5] For the earliest Christians, there was a link between renunciation of the world and its demonic beings and entry into the church where Jesus was Lord with his good angels. At the very core of becoming a Christian was the battle and thus the renunciation of the enemy and entry into the victory of Jesus. Cyril of Jerusalem, another early Christian theologian, told those who were about to be baptized that "each one of you is about to be presented to God *before tens of thousands of the angelic hosts*."[6]

Some of this is perhaps confusing to modern ears, which have silenced the hum of angels in a "contented worldliness," but the apostle Paul's words remind us that there is a battle that continues, the good angels are our advocates and Jesus has won the war. God's "intent was that now, through the church, the manifold wisdom of God [in Christ, through the cross and resurrection] should be made known to the *rulers and authorities in the heavenly realms*."* We need more than some wispy seraphs with horns atrumpeting or chubby cherubs smiling their way to our hearts to triumph over these bad angels. What we need is some fierceness in the angels. Our next theme will discover that fierceness.

---

* Ephesians 3:10

Part 4

God's Loving Transformation Through Angels

ANGELS JUDGE

I repeat the central lines in the Bible regarding angels, keeping in mind that every line is poured out from the God of love:

> God is Love.
>> All that God does is loving.
>> God sends angels to us because God loves us.
>> Love is a rugged commitment to be *With,*
>> to be *For* us so that we can
>> progress *Unto* Christlikeness.
>
>> Angels are sent to express God's love
>> by being God's presence with us,
>> by being God's presence for us, and
>> to lead us *into* the redemption of Christlikeness.

God loves us and that means God commits to be *with* us and to be *for* us, and this love of God is transformative. It leads *unto* Christlikeness. God loves us so much he will make us Christlike. This is not coercion but rather the transformative power of God's love. To be in God's presence is to be transformed by that presence. To have God on our side as our advocate is to be transformed by that presence. God's transformative presence leads us to the center of God's love, to the Son of God, and to our own Christlikeness.

No one who encounters an angel is ever the same afterward. We see this again and again in the Bible. Jacob is never the same after encountering angels ascending and descending. Ezekiel's vision within visions made him unfit for the world of Israel; he became a man possessed by a vision so grand he could not be satisfied with this life. And Mary, once she was told that her son would be the Messiah, was transformed into a completely different kind of person. She was no longer "Mary daughter of So-and-So" but always "Mary, mother of Jesus."

Angels are sent on mission to lead us into the transformation of redemption. Or as Jane Williams, author of a more-than-ordinary book about angels, once put it, angels are sent "to move us on, to help us to make some imaginative leap or overcome some mental hurdle that is preventing us from seeing what the world might be like and what our own role in it might be."[1]

I'd like to provide the contours of the transformative, redemptive process of angel encounters. God created us, along with myriads of angels and spiritual beings. At times God sends angels on mission to keep us on mission, to be with us and to be for us. But God's design from the beginning is to *transform* us so that we become Christlike. Likewise, angels are sent to transform us into Christlikeness.

One way they carry out the redemptive work of transformation is contained in the fierce word *judgment.* This word makes some of us hop backward a step and then sideward a step or two or perhaps duck. But the fact is that judgment is needed because the Bible treats evil as real and sinister and unwilling to change. Evil has one motivation: to destroy all life. So if we want to see God's love-sent angels do the work of transformation, we need to let them do what God sends them to do, which is to rid the world of sin, evil, injustice, and death.

An Impossible-to-Ignore but Still Ignored Theme

For the mission of the angels, namely, our redemption, to be accomplished, *all things* must be made right. For all things to be made right, judgment must come. For judgment to occur, evil must be defeated and those who choose the side of evil must be banished from the world of redemption. In the Bible, angels accomplish all this. At times they are sent on mission to announce or to execute judgment on evil and evil persons.

From the earliest prophets to the book of Revelation, from Elijah to the apostle John, two themes stand together and they fall together. You can't have one without the other: God's salvation is coming, and when that happens *God will judge evil by putting it away.* Angels are sent on mission to participate in that kind of redemption. For those who suffer, the message that angels are sent for judgment is very close to the best news they could imagine. "May it be!" is quickly followed by "And the sooner the better!"

ANGELS SENT TO CRACK DOWN ON EVIL

Cracking down on evil and evildoers is no assignment for chubby cherubs. Angels in the Jewish world were instruments of judgment. Jewish texts sometimes depict them as constant recorders of deeds. Here is a text not from the Bible, but rather from the *Apocalypse of Zephaniah,* that describes angels of judgment as those who care, who are watching, and who are recording the results of human behavior.

> Then I saw two other angels weeping over the three sons of Joatham, the priest. I said, "O angel, who are these?" He said, "These are the angels of the Lord Almighty. They write down all the good deeds of the righteous upon their manuscript as they watch at the gate of heaven. And I take them from their hands and bring them up before the Lord Almighty; he writes their name in the Book of the Living. Also the angels of the accuser who is upon the earth, they also write down all of the sins of men upon their manuscript. They also sit at the gate of heaven. They tell the accuser and he writes them upon his manuscript so that he might accuse them when they come out of the world (and) down there."*

---

* Apocalypse of Zephaniah 3:5–9

This text is apocryphal, and I'm not sure angels do this. But it is important to recall that this is how Jews at the time of Jesus thought about angels. Before we get to the major themes about angels as spirits sent on mission for judgment, I want to sketch a number of Bible references where this theme appears.

The first reference to angels in the Bible is found in Genesis 3:24, which describes angels standing guard with the flaming sword of warning and judgment, as if announcing "Do Not Enter Here!" In the famous Passover chapter in Exodus (chapter 12), we read of the avenging angel who slays the firstborn of the households that do not have blood on the door. In their wanderings through the wilderness to the land (see Exodus 23:20–21), the children of Israel are led by God's special angel. They are warned if they don't heed the angel's guidance they will not be forgiven. This same angel will lead them to victory over other nations. In chapter 24 of 2 Samuel, we learn of an angel that sent a plague of judgment that led to deaths, and we read a similar story in 2 Kings, chapter 19.

David once "looked up and saw the angel of the LORD standing between heaven and earth, *with a drawn sword in his hand extended over Jerusalem*."* Just in case you think this is restricted to Old Testament events, listen to the book of Acts:

> Immediately, because Herod did not give praise to God, an angel of the Lord struck him down, and he was eaten by worms and died.†

Do we need to mention how angel-filled the judgments of the book of Revelation are? We need to see the Bible's angels as flaming seraphs, swords in hands, sent on mission to rid the world of evil so that justice, peace, and love can flourish in the world God will redeem.

NOT JUST IN THE BIBLE

Angels can be agents of judgment. But just as often, they warn of judgment and summon the people of God to repentance.

---

* 1 Chronicles 21:16
† Acts 12:23

Here is a journal entry from someone detailing an angel appearance:

In May 1563 an angel dressed in white began appearing to Anna Schützin, the downtrodden wife of a common labourer from the village of Dürrmenz in the Duchy of Württemberg. The angel denounced the hardened hearts of rich men and assured her that God's anger was rising toward them. In the weeks that followed, the spirit continued to appear to Anna, urging her to tell her pastor to encourage his flock to repent. . . .

Word circulated, too, that on Friday 9 July Anna was to preach in the local church, and on that day, about 1,500 pilgrims flocked to hear her story. Frightened by such notoriety, Schützin refused to speak, and instead hid from the crowds, who had brought gifts of money if she proved willing to answer their questions. In the aftermath of the strange events at Dürrmenz, the local pastors continued to believe Schützin's story, while members of the more influential higher Lutheran clergy in the region doubted its authenticity.[2]

That journal entry dates to the year 1563. As I did research for this book, I read hundreds of stories about angels, and I have to admit to experiencing some melancholy over theme shifts in the last century and in this century. The messages ascribed to angels have turned soft and gentle and ever-so-positive. Yes, it is true that some have heard the hum of the angels of judgment and have not told their story to avoid being judged. This must be our reminder: angels often are sent to declare God's judgment of evil, and we live in a world that needs to hear the hum of that message.

Important Themes for the Angels of Judgment

The theme of angels as instruments of judgment, sent by God, grows in the Bible.[*] The final purpose of God is not punishment, nor is it retribution. God aims to restore all creation through the power of the resurrection. But that means God will

---

[*] A selection of Bible verses on this topic includes Joshua 5:13–14; Judges 6:11–21; 2 Samuel 24:15–17; 2 Kings 19:35; Acts 12:23; Matthew 13:38–39, 41–43, 49–50; Luke 12:8–9; Jude 14–15; Revelation 3:5; 12:7.

judge evil, abolish evil, and make us all new for the new creation. God's judgment opens the way for justice, for peace, for reconciliation, for healing, and for new creation. None of that can appear until judgment occurs. And in judgment we find the vigorous participation of angels.

Sometimes sin is so bad or injustice so pervasive that God intervenes through an angel to bring death. God purposes to restore creation, humans, and God's people. But sometimes sins are bad enough that death must occur for restoration to begin. The Bible includes scenes where an angel—a spirit on mission *from God,* we need to remind ourselves—is sent to bring the judgment of death.*

Sometimes the sin revealed by the angel is the complicated sin of leaders. There is a horrible story of death around David. We read of cringeworthy amounts of death that come by way of angelic destruction. This leads to David's repentance for his own evil.† His people suffered because of his sin. There is a matching story about Assyrian deaths in response to the prayer request of Hezekiah, king of Judah, and executed at the hand of the Angel of Yhwh. This episode is just as cringe-worthy and just as anchored in the pervasiveness of sin, idolatry, and blasphemy.‡ Angels sometimes have to deal death so that redemption can come into view.

Jesus announced that at times angels would execute final judgment. Notice Jesus's statements regarding angelic involvement in death-dealing judgment on sin, systemic evil, and selfish destruction:§

The field is the world, and the good seed stands for the people of the kingdom. The weeds are the people of the evil one, and the enemy who sows them is the devil. The harvest is the end of the age, and the harvesters are angels. . . .

The Son of Man will send out his angels, and they will weed out of his kingdom everything that causes sin and all who do evil. They will throw them into the blazing furnace, where there will be weeping and gnashing of

---

* For example, Judges 6:11–21; 2 Samuel 24:1
† 2 Samuel 24
‡ 2 Kings 19:15, 33–35
§ Matthew 13:38–39, 41–43, 49–50; Luke 12:8–9. If Jude is Jesus's brother as the church has always taught, then Jude 14–15 confirms the teachings of Jesus.

teeth. Then the righteous will shine like the sun in the kingdom of their Father. Whoever has ears, let them hear. . . .

This is how it will be at the end of the age. The angels will come and separate the wicked from the righteous and throw them into the blazing furnace, where there will be weeping and gnashing of teeth.

I tell you, whoever publicly acknowledges me before others, the Son of Man will also acknowledge before the angels of God. But whoever disowns me before others will be disowned before the angels of God.

One can't wish this theme away by pretending it's found only in the Old Testament. Jesus knows well the penetrating and pervasive depths of systemic evil in our world, and it is Jesus who lets us know that God will intervene through angels to execute the end of sin and evil. Only then will goodness and justice be forever established for all God's people. In the early church it was one of God's spirits on mission, an angel, who brought death to the violent, Christian-murdering Herod Agrippa.*

Sometimes we need to be reminded that a battle is being waged and we are in it whether we know it or not. The book of Revelation teaches the larger picture of the cosmic war that comes to its final battle.†

Then war broke out in heaven. Michael and his angels fought against the dragon, and the dragon and his angels fought back.

We looked at the cosmic battle in the previous chapter, so for now we need only a brief reminder that there are two teams, one captained by Michael and the other by the evil dragon. Each captain leads an army of angels into battle. The good news is that the decisive victory was achieved when Jesus crossed enemy lines, allowed the enemy to flay him on the cross, but then reversed their murderous glee when God raised him from death to rule over all powers. The war has been won, but the final

---

* Acts 12:23
† Revelation 12:7

battle has not yet begun. When the battle is over, it will be clear that the angels have been sent on mission to bring home the victory.

For the Transformation of Redemption to Occur

There will be no final transformation or redemption until all sin has been vanquished, until evil becomes a barely detectable echo down the long corridor of history, and until all evil persons have been defeated. Longing for that day of the new creation is central to the Bible. Angels sing in joy over that day. Hence, they are more than eager to share with God in judgment against sin and evil so it can be put away and the Great Dance of Eternity can begin. That will be the ultimate liberation from sin and evil, but here too is a surprise from the angels: that liberation has already begun.

ANGELS LIBERATE

One of the most important terms found in the Bible is *salvation* or *save,* which can be translated in some contexts as "rescue," "escape," or "liberate." Hence, the Bible's message of salvation is a message of liberation from danger, from opposition, from sin, from Satan, from systemic evil and injustice, and from self. But make no mistake, God's liberating work is holistic and so cannot be reduced to the spiritual dimension. God wants to set us free completely. One more time we must turn to the Bible's core themes about the angels: God loves us and because of that love God sends angels for our liberation.

A MISSIONARY PROTECTED AND LIBERATED TO CONTINUE GOSPEL MINISTRY

Billy Graham, the twentieth century's most influential evangelical and worldwide evangelist, told this story about an angel's liberation and protection. The story has to do with John G. Paton, a missionary. Here we see angels doing the work of protection to liberate the Patons for gospel work:

> Hostile natives surrounded his mission headquarters one night intent on burning the Patons out and killing them. John Paton and his wife prayed all during that terror-filled night that God would deliver them. When daylight

came they were amazed to see that, unaccountably, the attackers had left. They thanked God for delivering them.

A year later, the chief of the tribe was converted to Jesus Christ, and Mr. Paton, remembering what had happened, asked the chief what had kept him and his men from burning down the house and killing them. The chief replied in surprise, "Who were all those men you had with you there?" The missionary answered, "There were no men there; just my wife and I." The chief argued that they had seen many men standing guard—hundreds of big men in shining garments with drawn swords in their hands. They seemed to circle the mission station so that the natives were afraid to attack. Only then did Mr. Paton realize that God had sent His angels to protect them. The chief agreed that there was no other explanation.[1]

God sends angels to liberate us from the dark forces of death that take root in humans who oppose the mission of God.

THE FIRST LIBERATION OF PETER

That story about the Patons reminds me of a story we looked at earlier, the story of Lot's liberation from Sodom at the hand of angels.* In that episode, the Bible unleashes the beginning of a story about liberation, the premier liberation story being the exodus of the enslaved children of Israel from bondage in Egypt. Angels surround both of these events, reminding us that they are sent to carry out God's mission, and God's mission for this world is its liberation and redemption.

When it comes to Bible stories about liberation, my mind is captivated also by the story about the apostle Peter. Twice Peter was rescued from a Roman jail through the presence of an angel. First time: the apostolic ministry was proving hugely successful, so much so that Jerusalem's political leaders, called Sadducees, moved in and arrested Peter and other apostles. "But during the night," the book of Acts observes with more than a hint of excitement, "an angel of the Lord [the one who liberated

---

* Genesis 19

the children of Israel from Egypt] opened the doors of the jail and brought them out."*

The apostles resumed their successful preaching, but were it not for a peace-maker named Gamaliel, who intervened and asked the authorities to be more patient, death may have been dealt to each of the apostles. Instead of putting them to death, however, the authorities prohibited them from preaching (orders they disobeyed, of course) and then flogged them (which was painful, but was a source of joy for them because they participated in Jesus's sufferings). Peter was liberated by an angel from death to preach the gospel.†

Two Old Pastors Wondering

Novelist Marilynne Robinson wrote about churches and pastors in her *Gilead* trilogy. Two of Robinson's old heartland pastors, John Boughton and John Ames, in their waning years, frequently met to reminisce about life in Gilead.[2] Ames reminded Boughton of the time Boughton said, "What do you think you would do if you saw an angel?" Before Ames had a chance to respond, Boughton registered what he would do: "I'll tell you what, I'm scared I'd take off running!"

Now aged, he reiterated the answer, knowing his days of escape by running were over. "Well, I still might *want* to." Then added, because he felt his death looming: "Pretty soon I'll know." Old men pondering in a novel are not the real thing. But they are, I submit, *real-er* than the chubby cherub images so many of us have of angels. That is why Pastor Boughton thought an angel would frighten him. Which leads us to Peter's second liberation, where we will see fright.

The Second Liberation of Peter

Peter was liberated from jail a second time. In both liberations the angel empowered him to continue his vocation as an apostle.‡ The gospel was spreading into the

---

* Acts 5:19
† See Acts 5:17–41.
‡ This section all comes from Acts 12:1–19.

Gentile world, the church in Jerusalem was flourishing, a prophet announced a coming famine, and King Herod Agrippa I, grandson of the infamous Herod the Great, was fed up with the growth of the gospel and its threat to the established Jewish puppet authorities. Agrippa wanted to turn back the clock to the days when Jewish piety flourished free of the threat of this upstart movement. So he arrested some apostles. One of whom, James, brother of the apostle John, he murdered with a sword. When some of the established leaders approved of that execution, Agrippa decided to do the same to Peter, so he imprisoned the apostle. Evidently aware of what had happened the last time Peter was imprisoned in the Antonia Fortress near the temple, Herod stationed sixteen soldiers around Peter and saved him for a public trial following the feast of Passover.

What Agrippa did not know was that the church was praying and God was about to send another of his mighty angels into the mix to liberate Peter. What happened is eventful enough to read straight from the book of Acts:

> The night before Herod was to bring him to trial, Peter was sleeping between two soldiers, bound with two chains, and sentries stood guard at the entrance. Suddenly an angel of the Lord appeared and a light shone in the cell. He struck Peter on the side and woke him up. "Quick, get up!" he said, and the chains fell off Peter's wrists.
>
> Then the angel said to him, "Put on your clothes and sandals." And Peter did so. "Wrap your cloak around you and follow me," the angel told him. Peter followed him out of the prison, but he had no idea that what the angel was doing was really happening; he thought he was seeing a vision. They passed the first and second guards and came to the iron gate leading to the city. It opened for them by itself, and they went through it. When they had walked the length of one street, suddenly the angel left him.*

One moment Peter was surrounded by Roman soldiers and in chains, and the next moment an angel smacked him awake. Then he was walking free, and the next

---

* Acts 12:6–10

thing he knew the angel was gone. Standing alone in the middle of the street on a dark night and surely aware he could be in deep trouble for escaping, Peter came to his senses to perceive a powerful act of liberation. Unsure what to do, he went to a fellow apostle's house church and knocked on the door. After a confused greeter forgot protocol, the whole church turned to praise God for liberating Peter from prison to preach the gospel. This all came about through an angel.

A Reminder to Listen for the Hum of Angels

Some respond to stories such as those of Peter and of the protections of the Patons by dismissing them as hallucinations. Protestant Reformers often were critical of a spirituality that was open to experiences with angels. They urged caution and contained their discussions to what the Bible commanded. They emphasized God, Christ, and the Spirit, as well as the church, faith, and obedience. Their cautions often were seen as absolute prohibitions against admitting to or trusting any perception of having had a personal experience with an angel. Anyone who cares to explore Protestant church art will find that one of the impacts of the Reformation included stripping the altars and removing art from the walls of places of worship. This is especially visible in the later Puritan meetinghouses. That response to well-intended Christian art, as Alexandra Walsham has shown in her excellent study, reveals much. We hear about some church leaders tearing down images of Saint Michael and reducing the images to ashes in the churchyards![3]

Elizabeth Reis, a student of angels in church art, responded: "Angels were scarce in Calvinist New England." And with a little elbow to the ribs, added, "Angels appeared in the Bible but seemed rarely to venture abroad."[4] We are back to C. S. Lewis's "contented worldliness" when we fail to let the Bible's cosmic vision filled with angels and demons find its way into our minds, hearts, and art. Angels are active in our world in addition to their work that is recorded in the Bible.

ANGELS SEND ON MISSION

God has a mission for this world, one that takes us from creation into a testing ground to prepare us for the new heavens and the new earth. The mission is to transform this world from creation into the glories of the new creation.

To prepare us for new creation, God surprises some people with special messages that move the mission forward. At times God sends angels as spirits on mission to reveal what God's mission is or to remind us of that mission. At Northern Seminary, where I join wonderful colleagues in the mission of preparing leaders for the church, we have meetings during which someone (always) reminds us what we are doing—why we are here, what our aim is, why the seminary exists. One might detect the hum of angels over those conversations if one has an ear to listen.

I will draw our attention to three movement-reshaping moments of mission in the Bible where angels brought to the attention of key leaders the mission of God for the world. From these three moments of mission, we can draw an important thought: *whenever we remind ourselves of the mission of God, angels are present.* Once again, the Bible's core ideas about angels:

> God is Love.
>> All that God does is loving.
>> God sends angels to us because God loves us.
>> Love is a rugged commitment to be *With*,

to be *For* us so that we can
progress *Unto* Christlikeness.

Angels are sent to express God's love
by being God's presence with us,
by being God's presence for us, and
to lead us *into* the *missional calling of* redemption into
    Christlikeness.

MOSES: A MISSION REVEALED

The life and mission of Moses were reduced to the basics in a sermon delivered by a mighty hero in the Bible, Stephen.* Moses was called by God to rescue the children of Israel from slavery in Egypt and wasn't as patient waiting on God's timing as he should have been. Some forty years into his calling—and before anything had been accomplished (other than being personally prepared and prepared and prepared)—an angel appeared to Moses and revealed that God was and always had been present. So intense was God's "with-ness" that Moses was told to take off his shoes if he wanted to stand on such sacred space. God, through the angel, sent Moses to liberate the children of Israel. Here are Stephen's summary words:

He was sent to be their ruler and deliverer by God himself, *through the angel* who appeared to him in the bush. . . .

He was in the assembly in the wilderness, *with the angel* who spoke to him on Mount Sinai, and with our ancestors; and he received living words to pass on to us.†

Moses's fundamental mission—to be ruler and deliverer of Israel—was revealed through an angel. And since it was an angel on fire, we can assume the angel

---

* Acts 7:20–44
† Acts 7:35, 38

revealed itself as a seraph. We know Moses more as the lawgiver than perhaps we do as ruler and deliverer, but everything important about Moses's mission was revealed through the angel sent from God. If we assume the bookends of the Bible's grand story—from the Creation in Genesis to its completion in the new creation in the book of Revelation—a major chapter in the story is titled "Moses's Mission as Ruler, Deliverer, and Lawgiver." All of it revealed by angels.

Angels are sent on mission to communicate the mission and to keep us on mission.

ISAIAH: A MISSION REMINDER

Angels are spirits on the mission of redemption, and that redemption transforms us into Christlikeness. But that doesn't mean it's always happy-clappy. To be sure, nothing makes the chest swell like the angel-sent mission for Moses to liberate the children of Israel. From that moment on, enslaved people have known that God's mission is liberation. But sometimes the angel's mission from God is to reveal sin, to warn of judgment, and to bring destruction to tear down a nation's pride. Sometimes angels confront humans with a vision of God that takes more than their breath away.

Take Isaiah.* The great prophet of Israel is granted a vision of the Lord "high and exalted, seated on a throne; and the train of his robe filled the temple." Above him are six-winged seraphs crying out, "Holy, holy, holy is the LORD Almighty." When he encounters this vision, Isaiah crumbles into confession of his utter sinfulness. One of the seraphs comes to Isaiah with a "live coal" from the altar before God and touches Isaiah's lips to forgive him. We should pause here. The angel's mission is to exalt the holiness of God in such a manner that humans, even noble and courageous humans such as Isaiah, sense their *unworthiness and sinfulness*. Isaiah was transformed by this encounter.

Inherent in God's mission in the world is that we be reminded of who God is and that we catch a vision of God's beautiful holiness. There's more. The mission includes that we be reminded of how far we fall short and of how great and good

---

* I quote from Isaiah 6:1, 3, 6.

God is in his grace and forgiveness. The seraphs' mission leads to Isaiah's forgiveness.

Once forgiven, Isaiah is present when God asks who is ready to go on mission. Isaiah indicates his availability, so God sends the prophet to reveal to Israel that it, too, is sinful and in need of repentance and restoration. Otherwise, Israel will not be prepared to enter into new-creation realities.

Isaiah's message to Israel is anything but cheery. In short, it concerns the downfall of the nation and the sobering news that only the faithful will remain. Isaiah must announce judgment against the nation for its sinfulness. He must announce that they, like the tribes of northern Israel, will end up in exile (this time in Babylon), and that they, like the children of the northern kingdom, will find redemption in a new kind of exodus.

God sent Israel to tell the world about how new creation can come. Only the Israelites who believed Isaiah's message were transformed. God's mission, then, is not just to redeem Israel as God's special people, but also to redeem Israel for the sake of the world. They are, to use the words of Christopher Wright, "elected into mission."[1]

CHURCHES PRAYING ABOUT THE MISSION OF TRANSFORMATION

Whether church congregations today hear the hum of angels or not, angels are participating in the faithful mission of the church. Here is a story told by Chris:[2]

> The church was in one of the poorest neighborhoods in my home city of Brisbane, Australia. There were many people in the area who got mixed up in occult practices, usually teenagers and young adults who were close to homeless.
>
> A group of these kids made a practice of stealing small items from the church property to mark them somehow, symbolizing their ownership of the church and to "pray" against the church. Over the years, a few of these kids actually came to be Christians and told the church folks some pretty

amazing stories. One of them said that one day, when they were trying to steal a brick from the paved sidewalk outside the church, there were soldiers of light all around the building, guarding the place, and the kids ran away in terror.

Our church prayed regularly (given this kind of context and our mission to reach them) for God to set his angels around the place. So the story was one they told often.

Which leads us back to angels sent on mission to keep us on mission.

ANGELS AND THE EARLY CHRISTIAN MISSION

No one has mapped the impact of angels on early Christian mission any better than Jonathan Macy, who has detailed five different moments when angels sent the apostles on mission.

In the opening chapter of the book of Acts, after Jesus commissioned the apostles to spread out from Jerusalem into the whole of the Roman Empire, Jesus ascended into heaven. That is when the gawking apostles encountered an angel. The angel asked a finger-pointing question: "Why do you stand here looking into the sky?"[*] The implication being "Get on with it!"

Here's a second commissioning: apostles liberated from prison were sent on mission with these words: "Go, stand in the temple courts and tell the people all about this new life [= resurrection]."[†] A third: when the Ethiopian was on the way home from Jerusalem and searching for spiritual resolution in Isaiah, it was nothing other than an angel that instructed Philip to explain the gospel to the Ethiopian.[‡] A fourth, about Cornelius, we will look at in the next section. And we already looked at Peter's two releases from prison at the hands of angels. Finally, Macy takes us to Paul on his way to Rome, on mission but in Roman custody and in the midst of a shipwreck. Paul speaks these words about the mission:

---

* Acts 1:11
† Acts 5:20
‡ Acts 8:26–40, especially verses 26 and 39, where it shifts from angel to the Spirit of God.

Last night an angel of the God to whom I belong and whom I serve stood beside me and said, "Do not be afraid, Paul. You must stand trial before Caesar; and God has graciously given you the lives of all who sail with you." So keep up your courage, men, for I have faith in God that it will happen just as he told me.*

The angels seemed to show up at crucial mission moments. The apostles were never the same again, the church was never the same again, and all of this was set in motion through the mission of angels to conform us to the image of Christ and his mission.

Sad to say, far too many angel stories today have nothing to do with the mission of Christ. So, to stay faithful to the Bible, we return to the mission of God, the angels, and their being sent to keep us on mission.

PETER AND CORNELIUS

There was something in God's mission that Peter did not know. As a typical Jew, he had fallen into the trap of thinking election meant Israel was the *only* people of God. He needed to learn that God was at work everywhere and in everyone. To get Peter to see this—and you need to read Acts chapters 10 and 11 to get the full flavor—God sent an angel to a Roman military leader named Cornelius stationed in Caesarea. Cornelius was pious and reverent toward the God of Israel. The angel told Cornelius about Peter and sent him to visit Peter and then bring him back to Cornelius's home.

Not long after that, the angel appeared to Peter in Joppa and revealed in a vision that God was about to do something new. Peter was given this message in a very non-Jewish way: he was told to eat nonkosher food! Surely this is a parable to help Peter see that God's mission, from creation to new creation, is for the whole world. This revealed that God loves the kosher *and* the nonkosher.

Peter went to Caesarea and there told a crowd of people that God had shown

---

* Acts 27:23–25

him he was not to call unclean what God calls clean. (Again, insider Jewish talk for God expanding the people of God to include Gentiles in the new-creation mission.) Once Cornelius explained to Peter his visit with the angel, Peter said these magical words about God's mission. Note that this is the first-ever gospel sermon aimed *just at Gentiles:*

> I now realize how true it is that God does not show favoritism but accepts
> from every nation the one who fears him and does what is right.*

God's mission is to redeem people from around the world. Peter realized this because of his very Jewish vision involving unclean animals and because when he told the Gentiles around Cornelius about Jesus, they responded in repentance, faith, and baptism. What's more, they experienced the fullness of the Holy Spirit. Neither Peter nor Cornelius would ever be the same again. For both of them, this was a life- and mission-transforming encounter with the angels sent on mission from God.

The gospel began to abound in the Roman Empire as God, through his Spirit, drew people to Jesus. This event of expanding the mission of God to include Gentiles was prompted by an angel who visited a *Gentile Roman centurion!* Angels are spirits on mission sent to prompt humans to enter more deeply into God's mission from creation to new creation.

Hence they are especially concerned with churches.

ONE ANGEL PER CHURCH?

The book of Revelation tends to attract people who lean toward wild readings, wild ideas, and wild schemes for how history will unfold. Its wildness is its weakness for wild sorts of people. But that same wildness is its strength for those who surrender to its message. Revelation beautifully captures the central theme of the Bible: God is reclaiming his rule over this world. Through his Son he will put a full end to all evil and injustice, and he will establish his people in the new heavens and the new earth,

---

* Acts 10:34–35

a place flowing with love, justice, and peace. God's people will be centered on worshiping God through the Lamb's victory.[3]

Angels zip around everywhere in the Revelation because, as we have shown, they are spirits sent on mission. Wherever God's mission is on display, angels are watching and participating, which means they care about churches. So much is this the case that the book of Revelation assigns an angel to each church in Asia Minor. We might not be wrong in thinking God has sent an angel to every church in the world. Notice these Bible references, and even though it is repetitive, read each of them because there's something vital to what is said:[*]

> The mystery of the seven stars that you saw in my right hand and of the seven golden lampstands is this: The seven stars are *the angels of the seven churches,* and the seven lampstands are the seven churches.
>
> *To the angel of the church in Ephesus* write: These are the words of him who holds the seven stars in his right hand and walks among the seven golden lampstands.
>
> *To the angel of the church in Smyrna* write: These are the words of him who is the First and the Last, who died and came to life again.
>
> To *the angel of the church in Pergamum* write: These are the words of him who has the sharp, double-edged sword.
>
> To *the angel of the church in Thyatira* write: These are the words of the Son of God, whose eyes are like blazing fire and whose feet are like burnished bronze.
>
> To *the angel of the church in Sardis* write: These are the words of him who holds the seven spirits of God and the seven stars. I know your deeds; you have a reputation of being alive, but you are dead.
>
> To *the angel of the church in Philadelphia* write: These are the words of him who is holy and true, who holds the key of David. What he opens no one can shut, and what he shuts no one can open.
>
> To *the angel of the church in Laodicea* write: These are the words of the Amen, the faithful and true witness, the ruler of God's creation.

* Revelation 1:20; 2:1, 8, 12, 18; 3:1, 7, 14

Seven churches, seven angels. One angel per church. Could it be that God has assigned one angel to every church throughout history? Origen, the church's first full-blown theologian, was in the majority when he wrote about pastors (whom he called "bishops"), "there are two bishops in each church, one visible, the other invisible, and that both are busied with the same task."[4] One angel bishop and one human bishop, one angel per church.

Our problem is that we fail to listen for the hum of the angels that surround us, and therefore we call into question such a divine assignment for every church. Does not the Bible give us an entirely different impression? Namely, because angels surround us, we could far more biblically be saying, "Of course each church has an angel!" If the Bible teaches that each nation has an angel (as we clarified earlier), then it makes more than a little sense for each church to have an angel. If every church has an angel, we can be comforted that God has taken direct action for us. Angels care about all that happens in our churches, and angels are guarding and revealing God's ways to us. In other words, with Jesus as head of the whole church and therefore of each church, God has sent angels on mission to lead each of our churches into the depths of God's mission.

One more time: angels are sent on mission to communicate to us God's mission and to keep us on mission. Their mission is that we might be transformed.

22

ANGELS INTERCEDE

Angels continually worship the God who created the world and all its humans. They worship the God who loves those whom God has created—humans! In the midst of their worship, we also hear that angels intercede for humans. If the ultimate bad angel, Satan, comes before God to *accuse humans of sin,* it makes sense that the good angels intercede for us before God.

ANGELS, OUR PASTORAL INTERCESSORS IN THE OLD TESTAMENT

We see both types of angels in action in the opening passages of the book of Job. Satan stands as Job's accuser. At the same time, we are led to see good angels as intercessors.

Some of us need to be more suspicious of teachings that give too much weight to mediation between God and humans. Consider that the Reformers protested strongly against the Roman Catholic Church's creation of so many mediators: saints, angels, priests, statues, paintings, confessionals, indulgences, acts of contrition and penance, and fasts. The protest was needed. Suspicions at times lead to an overreaction because some of us need to see that angels intercede for us every moment of every day. We are not on our own, and that's a very, very good thing to know.

Read these words about our angel intercessors:

Yet if there is an angel at their side,

>   a messenger, one out of a thousand,

>   sent to tell them how to be upright,

and he is gracious to that person and says to God,

>   "Spare them from going down to the pit;

>   I have found a ransom for them—

let their flesh be renewed like a child's;

>   let them be restored as in the days of their youth"—

then that person can pray to God and find favor with him,

>   they will see God's face and shout for joy;

>   he will restore them to full well-being.*

Here the angels prepare God for our intercessions. Yes, we can go directly to God, but we might need to acknowledge that angels are already there, interceding. No, God is not being softened up by the angels in advance of our prayers. Rather, angels are doing what we *ought to want to do*. So we can take comfort in their intercession. We take comfort that angels, like human friends who pray for us, also care about our good.

Here's another instance of angels interceding, this time from the prophet Zechariah. Please read it carefully.

During the night I had a vision, and there before me was a man mounted on a red horse. He was standing among the myrtle trees in a ravine. Behind him were red, brown and white horses.

>   I asked, "What are these, my lord [= an angel]?"

>   The angel who was talking with me answered, "I will show you what they are."

Angels are scouting the world and reporting back to God on behalf of us humans. (This is an act of intercession.)

---

* Job 33:23–26

Then the man standing among the myrtle trees explained, "They are the ones the Lord has sent to go throughout the earth."

And they reported to the angel of the Lord who was standing among the myrtle trees, "We have gone throughout the earth and found the whole world at rest and in peace."

There follows an act of intercession by the angel in light of that report; and the angel reports to Zechariah the good news of God's mercy:

> Then the angel of the Lord said, "Lord Almighty, how long will you withhold mercy from Jerusalem and from the towns of Judah, which you have been angry with these seventy years?" So the Lord spoke kind and comforting words to the angel who talked with me.*

It is only because we refuse to listen for the hum of angels that we might find this type of intercession troubling. So let's back up: God created the heavens (filled with angels) and the earth (filled with humans). God's angels care about us, and that is because God created them to be his servants.

Here is what we will consider at length: because angels care about fellow creatures such as us, they intercede for us in God's presence. We can expand this to include one more element: they take our intercessions and lay them before God. The book of Revelation shows the sort of intercessions most humans in history have had and makes it clear that angels are holding our prayers before our Father.

ANGELS, OUR PASTORAL INTERCESSORS IN THE NEW TESTAMENT

A wonderful passage in Revelation illustrates how our prayers are given *advocacy* by angels surrounding God's throne.

---

* Zechariah 1:8–13

And I saw the seven angels who stand before God, and seven trumpets were given to them.

Another angel, who had a golden censer, came and stood at the altar. He was given much incense to offer, with the prayers of all God's people, on the golden altar in front of the throne. The smoke of the incense, together with the prayers of God's people, went up before God from the angel's hand.*

The seven angels probably are the seven named archangels well known in the Jewish tradition.[1] At least many believing Jews who read this text would think immediately of those seven archangels. But John stated that "another angel" had a golden censer, a pan filled with coals and incense that was carried before the altar or throne. The incense is a symbol for the prayers of the saints, and it is an angel that lays this incense before God. Thus, the angel reminds God and in doing so enhances the prayers of the saints.

Instead of being troubled by the intercession of angels, we need to be comforted to know they are already doing what we might need to learn to do.

ANGELS ADVOCATING FOR JUSTICE AND PEACE

In the book of Revelation, the saints are shown to be crying out for justice and peace because they are experiencing intense persecution, even martyrdom. Their prayers are sometimes "How long?" or, with perhaps a sharper punctuation, "How long!" Thus,

They called out in a loud voice, "How long, Sovereign Lord, holy and true, until you judge the inhabitants of the earth and avenge our blood?"†

The angel's task in that heavenly scene is to offer these prayer requests before God's throne—to remind, to enhance, and to illustrate the prayers of God's people for justice to be brought about. The good news is that God responds to the angel's action and we see this in what happens next:

---

* Revelation 8:2–4
† Revelation 6:10

Then the angel took the censer, filled it with fire from the altar, and hurled it on the earth; and there came peals of thunder, rumblings, flashes of lightning and an earthquake.*

This act unleashes God's judgment against injustice by eliminating injustice and, in its place, restoring the world to justice and peace and reconciliation. The wrath of the angels in Revelation ends not with punishment but with a new creation, the new heavens and the new earth.

Every moment of injustice in our world is punctuated with a prayer for justice by God's people, and it leads to angels tapping their fingers on the table and shuffling their feet and running their eyes to and fro in the hope that God will send them to restore the world to God's true mission. These angels want to act in judgment against evil and injustice because the true mission of the angels is to transform the cosmos. They know God's mission, they know their part in it, and they know our part. That redemptive mission will transform God's people and transform God's world into the new heavens and the new earth.

When that happens, and it will, all creation will join the angels and archangels in singing praise to God in endless worship. The redemptive mission of the angels, nothing less than God's expression of his love and grace for us, will be complete when we are transformed to spend eternity *with* the God who has always been *for* us so that we might be transformed *unto* Christlikeness. That last stage of redemption will be filled with angels.

Here then are the major lines about angels in the Bible:

God is Love.
    All that God does is loving.
    God sends angels to us because God loves us.
    Love is a rugged commitment to be *With*,
    to be *For* us so that we can
    progress *Unto* Christlikeness.

---

* Revelation 8:5

Angels are sent *from their life of worship and intercession*
   to express God's love
by being God's presence with us,
by being God's presence for us, and
to lead us into the redemption of Christlikeness.

23

ANGELS LEAD IN WORSHIP

Praise and worship, these are what the "archetypal adorers of God"[1] do. They lead us to praise and worship God. Keep in mind that before angels are sent on mission to keep us on mission, they are worshiping God. In fact, their mission arises from their worship. And once they complete a mission, they reenter the circle of worship surrounding God's throne.

The Bible's story about angels follows a familiar arc. Summoned from their worship to communicate with us about God's mission, they fulfill their mission and then return to worship. *Anything then that we experience about angels ought to derive from and lead to worship of God.*[2] As T. F. Torrance once said, "Just as angels do not draw attention to themselves but point away to the Lord who has sent them as his messengers and witnesses, so their function among us is *to direct our attention away from ourselves to glorify God alone* in the highest."[3]

WORSHIP AS REDEMPTION'S GOAL

Angels are sent on mission to communicate with us and to keep us on mission with a goal toward our total redemption. Complete redemption means we become worshipers of God. We might ask what worship is. A famous theologian of worship, William Temple, once defined worship.

Worship is the submission of all our nature to God. It is the quickening of our conscience by His holiness; the nourishment of our mind with His truth; the purifying of the imagination by His beauty; the opening of the heart to His love; the surrender of the will to His purpose, and all this gathered up in adoration, the most selfless emotion of which our nature is capable.[4]

Wow, it doesn't get any better than that. Angels are sent to transform us into that kind of worship. Here, again, is our map that lays out the scope of the mission of angels:

God is Love.
    All that God does is loving.
    God sends angels to us because God loves us.
    Love is a rugged commitment to be *With,*
    to be *For* us so that we can
    progress *Unto* Christlikeness.

    Angels are sent *from their life of worship and intercession*
        to express God's love
    by being God's presence with us,
    by being God's presence for us, and
    to lead us into the redemption of Christlikeness,
    which at its heart is the worship of God forever and ever!

ANGELS AND WORSHIP IN JEWISH AND EARLY CHRISTIAN PRACTICE

Perhaps the most common Bible-related belief about angels in the ancient world was that they worshiped God. I will give two instances of this, one from a Jewish text prior to the New Testament and one from an early Christian text following the first century. It is time to take a peek at the Dead Sea Scrolls, in particular at a text now called "The Songs of the Sabbath Sacrifice." This text describes how some Jews imagined or experienced worship among the angels. It's a bit loaded and dense, but a patient reading will give at least a window on what people around Jesus and the apostles believed. The text is a kind of commentary on the vision of angels that Ezekiel experienced. We will encounter angels rising, blessing, singing, praising, and dancing to the beat of God's glory. And we will notice silence as well.

> The cherubs fall down before him, and bless. When they rise the murmuring sound of gods is heard, and there is an uproar of exultation when they lift their wings, the murmuring sound of gods. They bless the image of the throne-chariot (which is) above the vault of the cherubs, and they sing the splendour of the shining vault (which is) beneath the seat of his glory. And when the ophanim move forward, the holy angels return; they emerge from between its glorious wheels with the likeness of fire, the spirits of the holy of holies. Around them is the likeness of streams of fire like electrum, and a luminous substance gloriously multi-coloured, wonderful colours, purely blended. The spirits of living gods move constantly with the glory of the wonderful chariots. And (there is) a murmuring voice of blessing in the uproar of their motion, and they praise the holy one on returning to their paths. When they rise, they rise wonderfully; when they settle, they stand still. The sound of glad rejoicing becomes silent and there is a calm blessing of gods in all the camps of the gods. And the sound of praises . . . from among all their divisions on their sides . . . and all their enrolled ones exult, each one in his station.[5]

The view then, was that in the abode of God, there is silence flowing into worship flowing into a deep stillness.

In his splendid book on early-church spiritual practices, Andrew B. McGowan included a brief discussion of the oldest Christian hymn that is accompanied by musical notations. It is from about two hundred fifty years after Christ and here are the words, though the manuscript was not in good enough condition to preserve all the words. (The ellipses indicate where some words are no longer recoverable. The brackets indicate words that are surely implied.)

Together all the esteemed ones of God . . .

>   Let them be silent. Let the shining stars not . . .

>   . . . let the [rushings of winds, and springs] of all surging rivers
[cease.]

>   While we sing

>   Father and Son and Holy Spirit, let all the answering powers say "Amen,
Amen."

>   Might and praise

>   [always and glory to God,] the only giver of all good things, Amen. Amen.[6]

Perhaps you missed it, but that opening line, "all the esteemed ones of God," is a reference to summoning angels to participate in the worship of saints on earth. Angels are known for their singing. When J. R. R. Tolkien, in *The Silmarillion,* held that the angels sang the world into existence, he was drawing out what is found not only in the Jewish texts and the early Christian texts but also in the Bible.[7]

THE ANGELS WORSHIP GOD

At the moment of the creation of the universe or our solar system, regardless of how many years you usher it back, angels broke into praise of God's glorious energy and might, shown in God's turning nonmatter into matter. God once interrogated a man named Job, using the following words to humble him. What was Job in light of the vastness of God's immensity and power and grandeur?

>   Where were you when I laid the earth's foundation?

>   >   Tell me, if you understand.

>   Who marked off its dimensions? Surely you know!

>   >   Who stretched a measuring line across it?

>   On what were its footings set,

>   >   or who laid its cornerstone—

With that question God added this to color in what was happening when God created:

> while the morning stars sang together
>> and all the angels shouted for joy?*

At the moment when God created the universe, angels "sang together" and they "shouted for joy." These angels, the Bible tells us over and over, are intoxicated with worship of God. They have praised and worshiped God day and night for ages past and will continue to do so for eternity into the eternity of eternities:

> Ascribe to the LORD, you heavenly beings,
>> ascribe to the LORD glory and strength.

> In the council of the holy ones God is greatly feared;
>> he is more awesome than all who surround him.†

Not only do angels worship God, all creation is designed and encouraged to worship God.

THE ANGELS JOIN ALL CREATION IN WORSHIPING GOD

Here is one of Israel's favorite songs. It was repeated often enough that it was included in Israel's hymn book, the Psalms. In this psalm, we discover that praise of God joins angels to Israel's own worship team:

> Praise the LORD.
> Praise the LORD from the heavens;
>> praise him in the heights above.

---

* Job 38:4–7
† Psalm 29:1; 89:7

Praise him, *all his angels;*

praise him, all his heavenly hosts.

Praise him, sun and moon;

praise him, all you shining stars.

Praise him, you highest heavens

and you waters above the skies.

Let them praise the name of the LORD,

for at his command they were created,

and he established them for ever and ever—

he issued a decree that will never pass away.*

Whether we hear it in Christian hymns or in the Bible, or sense it in the grandeur of the Grand Canyon or the spacious Cliffs of Moher of the Republic of (western) Ireland, all creation sings praise to God. In light of all that has been said in this book, we would be more accurate to say that creation is being summoned to join the angelic chorus. This is more accurate than saying that angels join in the praise given by all of creation.

One of my favorite sacred hymns is called "Immortal, Invisible God Only Wise" and in that glorious hymn, which is meant to be sung with organ and a choir, we read these words: "thine angels adore thee, all veiling their sight."[8] Oh yes, the rich song traditions of Judaism and Christianity know an abundance of angels worshiping God, and for us Christians we know they worship Jesus himself.

THE ANGELS WORSHIP JESUS

The angels worship God Almighty, the God of creation, the God of Israel. *Therefore* when God becomes incarnate in Jesus as the Son of God and the Lamb of God, the angels of God worship Jesus too! They worshiped him the moment Jesus entered into the pages of history as a human:

---

* Psalm 148:1–6

And again, when God brings his firstborn into the world, he says,

"Let all God's angels worship him."*

Luke described this scene taking place when Jesus was born in Bethlehem:

Suddenly a great company of the heavenly host appeared with the angel, praising God . . . †

Second, angels worship in heaven as the key to history itself.

After this I looked, and there before me was a great multitude that no one could count, from every nation, tribe, people and language, standing before the throne and before the Lamb. They were wearing white robes and were holding palm branches in their hands. And they cried out in a loud voice:

"Salvation belongs to our God,
who sits on the throne,
and to the Lamb."

All the angels were standing around the throne and around the elders and the four living creatures. They fell down on their faces before the throne and worshiped God, saying:

"Amen!
Praise and glory
and wisdom and thanks and honor
and power and strength
be to our God for ever and ever.
Amen!"‡

---

* Hebrews 1:6
† Luke 2:13
‡ Revelation 7:9–12

These Bible references need to be tied together again. Angels are sent on mission to communicate God's mission and to keep us on mission. God's mission is redemption, and the center of that redemption is Jesus, the Lamb who was slain. His death slays death, and his resurrection conquers death and the devils of the world. Hence, we cannot be one bit surprised that the worshiping angels of God's presence worship the Lamb. And their mission is to lead us to do the same.

ANGELS ARE SENT TO LEAD US INTO WORSHIP

When I was a young boy, one of my heroes in the Bible was Samson. Athletic enough to play football and tall enough to play basketball and handsome enough to be on the homecoming court, the man seemed to have it all. But his story is kicked off with a surprising (pastoral) visit from an angel, who gives his mom and dad the best news possible. Here are words about Samson from the book of Judges:*

> A certain man of Zorah, named Manoah, from the clan of the Danites,
> had a wife who was childless, unable to give birth. *The angel of the* LORD
> appeared to her and said, "You are barren and childless, but you are going
> to become pregnant and give birth to a son. Now see to it that you drink
> no wine or other fermented drink and that you do not eat anything
> unclean. You will become pregnant and have a son whose head is never to
> be touched by a razor because the boy is to be a Nazirite, dedicated to God
> from the womb. He will take the lead in *delivering Israel* from the hands of
> the Philistines."

There's a lot to this encounter between Samson's father, Manoah, and his wife, and this angel (whom Manoah thinks is a man). But I want to skip ahead. In the middle of the conversation between the Angel of the LORD and Manoah, the angel said, "But if you prepare a burnt offering, offer it to the LORD." Manoah pled for the man's name, the angel refused. Now comes the cool part:

---

* The following quotations are from Judges 13:2–5, 16, 19–21.

Then Manoah took a young goat, together with the grain offering, and sacrificed it on a rock to the LORD. And the LORD did an amazing thing while Manoah and his wife watched: As the flame blazed up from the altar toward heaven, the angel of the LORD ascended in the flame. Seeing this, Manoah and his wife fell with their faces to the ground. When the angel of the LORD did not show himself again to Manoah and his wife, Manoah realized that it was the angel of the LORD.

Their response? Worship. Afterward, they were scared to death that they had seen God and were therefore deserving of death. But Manoah's wife had better theological sense. She said, "If the LORD had meant to kill us, he would not have accepted a burnt offering and grain offering from our hands, nor shown us all these things or now told us this."* Baby Samson was born, destined to be a Spirit-empowered, sometimes-righteous and sometimes-not-so-righteous, judge in Israel. Our concern here is not what became of Samson but the proper response to this glowing pastoral visit from an angel. The response is *worship.* God granted the parents a very special child. God revealed this through an angel experience that was slaked with miracle and power. The couple's response: they "fell with their faces to the ground."

The angels care about all creation worshiping God. In line with that, they lead us to worship the Lamb who is on the throne. Hence, they join humans in this Lamb-shaped worship. Notice how the elders in heaven (who are humans) sing praise to God for redemption. As the elders sing, the angels, like a chorus singing the refrain, join in on the worship. I have italicized the narrative highlights of this all-too-brief but glorious passage:

> Then I saw a *Lamb,* looking as if it had been slain, standing at the center
> of the throne, encircled *by the four living creatures and the elders.* . . . the
> four living creatures and the twenty-four elders fell down before the
> Lamb. Each one had a harp and they were holding golden bowls full

---

* Judges 13:23

of incense, which are the prayers of God's people. And they sang a new song, saying:

"You are worthy to take the scroll
     and to open its seals,
because you were slain,
     and with your blood you purchased for God
     persons from every tribe and language and people and nation.
You have made them to be a kingdom and priests to serve our God,
     and they will reign on the earth."

Then I looked and heard the voice of many angels, numbering thousands upon thousands, and ten thousand times ten thousand. They encircled the throne and the living creatures and the elders. In a loud voice they were saying:

"Worthy is the Lamb, who was slain,
     to receive power and wealth and wisdom and strength
     and honor and glory and praise!"*

In our church, nearly every Sunday of the year before we celebrate the Lord's Supper, we say these words with the seraphs of Isaiah (as we noted earlier). It is called a Preface with the Sanctus (Holy, Holy, Holy):

Therefore we praise you, joining our voices with Angels and Archangels and with all the company of heaven, who for ever sing this hymn to proclaim the glory of your Name:
     Holy, Holy, Holy Lord, God of power and might, heaven and earth are full of your glory. Hosanna in the highest. Blessed is he who comes in the name of the Lord. Hosanna in the highest.†

---

* Revelation 5:6–12
† *The Book of Common Prayer* (1990), 362.

There is no better place to end this book than with our joining the angels in worshiping God. That is the intent of redemption, and if someone were to wander into our church, I hope they'd feel welcome but also experience some vertigo—swarmed by angels spinning in their glory around the God of glory and drawing us heavenward.[9]

APPENDIX

THE SO-CALLED HIERARCHY OF ANGELS

The most influential book about angels in the history of the church was written by a person now called Pseudo-Dionysius. He wasn't known as "Pseudo" until centuries after the book was written. His compact little book is called *The Celestial Hierarchy*.[1] When I say "influential," I don't mean the author was right, but that his speculations about angels set off a history of thinking about angels based on his speculations about the hierarchy of heaven and its angels.

Though Pseudo-Dionysius has played an important role in one kind of angel studies in the church, before his work there existed many other sketches of the hierarchy of the spirits in heaven.[2] I will begin with his important work and then sketch out a few other supposed angel hierarchies. The more exposed we are to this kind of thinking about angels and what they are like and how many there are, the more we realize two things. First, how much we don't really know, and second, how much speculation has been involved even in what Christian theologians have said about angels. By the end of this appendix, I hope to show that we have no idea of the relation between and among the various spirits in the heavens. In reality, the so-called hierarchy is a castle of angels built in the air.

But because hierarchical thinking has been so influential, we need to spend some time explaining it.

AN ASSORTMENT OF HIERARCHIES

Pseudo-Dionysius organized heaven into three choirs of three angelic beings, which add up to nine levels of supernatural heavenly beings. The choirs, he wrote, are

God (Father, Son, Spirit).

The angelic world of celestial beings, in three choirs, are

First Choir of Angels:
Seraphim
Cherubim
Thrones[3]

Second Choir of Angels:
Dominions
Virtues
Powers

Third Choir of Angels:
Principalities
Archangels
Angels[4]

And finally, there are *Humans*

In what follows I hope to so thoroughly confuse the picture that we will realize talk about hierarchies is speculation and we ought to move on to what we can and should know about the beings in the heavenly places. Prior to the New Testament and in the world of Judaism, that is, between the Old Testament and the New Testament, there were other rankings. I begin with one from around the time of the New Testament, from a book called 1 Enoch.[5]

And these are names of the holy angels who watch:
Suru'el, one of the holy angels—for (he is) of eternity and of trembling.
Raphael, one of the holy angels, for (he is) of the spirits of man.
Raguel, one of the holy angels who take vengeance for the world and for the luminaries.

Michael, one of the holy angels, for (he is) obedient in his benevolence over the people and the nations.

Saraqa'el, one of the holy angels who are (set) over the spirits of mankind who sin in the spirit.

Gabriel, one of the holy angels who oversee the garden of Eden, and the serpents, and the cherubim.

That same book (1 Enoch) also gives names to four angels that manage the four seasons of the year (Malki'el, Hela'emmemelik, Milay'ul, Narel; 82:13). First Enoch sets forth but one such attempt to order the heavens. Another book from roughly the same time period, Jubilees, assigns various angels to various tasks:

For on the first day he created the heavens, which are above, and the earth, and the waters and all of the spirits which minister before him:

the angels of the presence,

and the angels of sanctification,

and the angels of the spirit of fire,

and the angels of the spirit of the winds,

and the angels of the spirit of the clouds and darkness and snow and hail and frost,

and the angels of resoundings and thunder and lightning,

and the angels of the spirits of cold and heat and winter and springtime and harvest and summer,

and all of the spirits of his creatures which are in heaven and on earth (Jubilees 2:2).

From a much later period we read in the rabbinical writings of another way of ordering the heavens and forming the spirits into a hierarchy. To begin with, one text says, "everything in the world exists in a hierarchy." It mentions the heavens, the earth, and the stars, as well as beasts, humans, and angels.[6] That seems reasonable. The great medieval Jewish scholar Maimonides, in his own moment of speculation, clarified the hierarchy for his readers with this:

There is a change of names of angels, according to their level. The highest
level consists of the *Holy Chayot* then come the *Ophanim,* the *Erelim,* the
Chashmalim, the *Seraphim,* the *Malachim,* the *Elohim,* the *Bnei Elohim,*
the *Cheruvim* and the *Ishim.* These are the ten names that the angels are
called by, according to their ten degrees.

    The highest level is that of the *Holy Chayot* and there is none other above
it, except that of God. Therefore, in the Prophecies, it is said that they are
underneath God's throne. The tenth level consists of the *Ishim,* who are the
angels who speak with the Prophets and appear to them in prophetic visions.
They are therefore called *Ishim* (men) because their level is close to the level
of the consciousness of human beings. [7]

Perhaps the modern world's most knowledgeable historian of angels, Valery
Rees, offers a commentary on this rabbinic text:

The *Chayot* and *Ophanim* are the Living Beings and Wheels of Ezekiel's
vision, and *Erelim* are Thrones. *Chashmal* is the mysterious substance in
Ezekiel's vision, sometimes translated as amber. *Seraphim* and *Cheruvim* are
more familiar . . . , and *Malachim* are the messenger angels we have already
met. Perhaps the *Cheruvim* appear so apparently low in the list because of
their presence among mankind, as for example on the cover of the Ark of the
Covenant. *Elohim* are undefined divine powers, but the use here echoes that
in the Qumran texts, meaning just "angels." The new category here is the
Bnei Elohim, their sons. Yet angels are created each for a specific task and do
not procreate—unless perhaps these may be the "sons of God" of Genesis
6:2? The last rank are the *Ishim,* and they derive their name from *Ish,* a
man."[8]

We may not all agree with Karl Barth, but at least he brought into expression
what many of us sense after reading this mishmash of speculations about a hierarchy
of angels. He wrote that Pseudo-Dionysius's celestial ranking was "one of the greatest
frauds in Church history."[9] Barth added wisely that this subject of angels for far too

many involves "a good deal of theological caprice, of valueless, grotesque and even absurd speculation."[10] I agree.

WHAT WE CAN KNOW ABOUT THE HIERARCHY OF HEAVEN

Let's stick to what the Bible actually says. God is above all and his Son is the Preeminent One over all creation. Below the Son are various spiritual beings, including angels. Here is how the apostle Paul put it:

> For in him all things were created: things in heaven and on earth, visible and invisible, whether thrones or powers or rulers or authorities; all things have been created through him and for him. He is before all things, and in him all things hold together.*

Christ is the creator and sustainer of all life, whether it is in the heavens or on earth. That heavenly realm, so it appears, is made up of the invisible realm. Paul gives these names with *no indication* of hierarchical ordering. The names are "thrones or powers or rulers or authorities."

On top of this, one can compose an even more complete list of names used for angelical beings: angels, sons of God, watchers, holy ones, hosts (or armies), the four living creatures, spirits, thrones, rulers, dominions, principalities, and powers.† We may have names of distinguishable sorts of supernatural beings, but their relationship to one another is left unclarified. One more fact about angels in the Bible: two archangels are named (Michael, Gabriel).‡ In the Apocrypha we get Raphael, so at least three are named in the Bible and its expansion for some Christians. But while this implies that these two or three are superior to ordinary angels, we don't learn a thing about their relationship to the other named beings of heaven.

Here's how I summarize what the Bible says:

---

* Colossians 1:16–17; see also Ephesians 1:19–21; 6:12
† Angel: Luke 2:9. Sons of God: Genesis 6:1–4; Job 1:6. Spirits: Hebrews 1:14. Holy Ones: Psalm 89:5, 7. Cherubs: Genesis 3:24. Seraphs: Isaiah 6:1–7. Archangels: Jude 9. Principalities and powers: Colossians 1:16 and see also 2:13–15.
‡ Daniel 10:13; Luke 1:19; Revelation 12:7

God is creator through Christ of all things, in the heavens and on earth.

God made spiritual beings for the heavenly realm.

These beings have various names; there is no clear order other than "archangels" and "angels."

God made humans for the earthly realm.

Barth may be too harsh, but at least we might agree with John Calvin, who wrote, "Therefore let us remember not to probe too curiously or talk too confidently."[11] He had mentioned a few pages earlier what applies most especially to much of what has been and is being said about angels: "The theologian's task is not to divert the ears with chatter, but to strengthen consciences by teaching things true, sure, and profitable."[12] I agree, so in *The Hum of Angels* I have sought to get down to the basics in what the Bible actually says. This prayer from *The Book of Common Prayer* will push us toward the shore:

Blessed Lord, who caused all holy Scriptures to be written for our learning: Grant us so to hear them, read, mark, learn, and inwardly digest them, that we may embrace and ever hold fast the blessed hope of everlasting life, which you have given us in our Savior Jesus Christ; who lives and reigns with you and the Holy Spirit, one God, for ever and ever. Amen. [13]

AFTER WORDS

To come to the end of a book is to come to the end of a chapter in life. I have thought about angels for a long time; sometimes they were humming ever so silently at the edge of my consciousness, at other times they jumped off the pages of the Bible, and at other times I was left wondering if I had perhaps just been in one's presence. Folks at times ask me what is the favorite book I have written, and my answer is always the same: "The last one." The intensity of study, prayer, discussion, reading, and writing tend to become more and more intense the closer I get to the end of a book. So much so that when I send the manuscript off to the editor and publisher, I miss the book the way I miss friends who have moved on. I write this after editorial suggestions and after moving on to some other projects, but I have missed *The Hum of Angels* more than I expected, and it doesn't help that I seem to see something about angels every day on the Internet.

Speaking of moving on, my graduate assistant for the last three years at Northern Seminary has been Tara Beth Leach. But she has now both graduated and become the senior pastor at First Church of the Nazarene in Pasadena, California. She was abundantly enthused about the subject of this book and contributed in numerous ways, not least through her diligence in finding materials for me to read. She also provided me with some stories that show up in this book, though the names of those who told them, apart from one person (Tara Beth herself), have been changed.

I also want to thank a world-class scholar on angels, Jonathan Macy, for reading the manuscript twice, for offering an endorsement of the book, and for his very thoughtful book on angels. My agent, Greg Daniel, has provided constant wisdom in the process of writing, not to ignore his fun-loving updates on Facebook. At WaterBrook I want to thank Andrew Stoddard for his enthusiasm and passion for this project and Ron Lee for his more than careful editorial suggestions. Both have made this book better than I deserve.

My colleague at Northern Seminary, Claude Mariottini, an Old Testament specialist, has answered not a few of my questions about angels, and I thank him. I offer my gratitude to both Karen Walker Freeburg, for her noble work as interim president, and now to William Shiell, our new president. They have both opened the kind of space needed for research and writing.

It is customary these days to attribute the word *angel* or *angelic* to those we love most, but as this book attempted to show, that usage of *angel* is not warranted in the Bible. But if there is such a person, it would be Kris, who listened over the past years to my angel chatter and who offered more than one piece of advice about this book that is now enshrined in its words.

Ordinary Time 2016
Scot McKnight

NOTES

Chapter 1: The Hum of Angels

1. Martin Israel, *Angels: Messengers of Grace* (London: SPCK, 1995), 41.
2. Jane Williams, *Angels* (Grand Rapids, MI: Baker Books, 2007), 124.
3. Emma Heathcote-James, *Seeing Angels* (London: John Blake, 2001), 148–150.
4. Emma Heathcote-James, *Seeing Angels*, 27–28.
5. Emma Heathcote-James, *Seeing Angels*, 226–27.
6. Andy Angel, *Angels: Ancient Whispers of Another World* (Eugene, OR: Wipf & Stock, 2012), 1.
7. Andy Angel, *Angels*, 14.
8. Mortimer J. Adler, *The Angels and Us* (New York: Touchstone, 1993); Peter S. Williams, *The Case for Angels* (Carlisle, UK: Paternoster, 2003). For a tight listing of consideration leading P. S. Williams to belief in angels, see his Appendix.
9. Some scholars debate which passages count as "angel" passages. The Bible uses terms such as *cherub* and *seraph* for invisible beings; at other times the Bible uses the term *angel*. It is fair to ask whether cherubs and seraphs are angels or something other than angels. I believe *angel* is a more generic term and that it includes cherubs and seraphs. Were I to agree with those who think cherubs and seraphs are not really angels in the technical sense, it would not make much difference to this book.
10. Claus Westermann, *God's Angels Need No Wings*, trans. David L. Scheidt (Philadelphia: Fortress, 1979), 12.
11. Westermann, *God's Angels Need No Wings*, 7.
12. Charles R. Jaekle, *Angels: Their Mission and Message* (Harrisburg, PA: Morehouse, 1995), 2. Italics added. The expression "spiritual underground" comes from Jaekle, 4.

13. Valery Rees, *From Gabriel to Lucifer: A Cultural History of Angels* (London: I. B. Tauris, 2013), 55–56.

14. The expression "shrug of the shoulders" was a favorite of Karl Barth's; see Karl Barth, *Church Dogmatics: The Doctrine of Creation,* ed. Geoffrey W. Bromiley and T. F. Torrance, Study Edition 18, vol. 3.3 (London: T & T Clark, 2010), 130.

Chapter 2: Most of Us Believe in Angels

1. Jane Williams, *Angels* (Grand Rapids, MI: Baker Books, 2007), 123.

2. Peter Marshall and Alexandra Walsham, "Migrations of Angels in the Early Modern Period," in *Angels in the Early Modern World* (Cambridge, UK: Cambridge University Press, 2006), 1–2.

3. Rodney Stark ed., *What Americans Really Believe: New Findings from the Baylor Surveys of Religion* (Waco, TX: Baylor University Press, 2008), 63, 90.

4. Emma Heathcote-James, *Seeing Angels* (London: John Blake, 2001), 12. For the report that claims one-third of us have seen an angel, see Nancy Gibbs, "Angels Among Us," *Time,* December 27, 1993. http://content.time.com/time/magazine /article/0,9171,979893,00.html.

5. Connie Cass, "AP-GfK Poll: Why Do Kids Have Faith in Santa?" AP-GfK, December 23, 2011, http://ap-gfkpoll.com/featured/ ap-gfk-poll-december-2011-santa-topline/.

6. Anthony McCarron, "Nick Swisher Honors Memory of Woman Who Raised Him," *Daily News,* May 9, 2009, www.nydailynews.com/sports/baseball /yankees/nick-swisher-honors-memory-woman-raised-article-1.409227/.

7. Bob Nightengale, "Nightengale: Royals Find Fitting End to World Series Title," *USA Today,* November 3, 2015, www.usatoday.com/story/sports/mlb/2015 /11/02/kansas-city-royals-world-series-championsip-game-5/75021956/.

8. Gerald R. McDermott, *The Great Theologians: A Brief Guide* (Downers Grove, IL: InterVarsity, 2010).

9. Karl Barth, *Church Dogmatics: The Doctrine of Creation,* ed. Geoffrey W. Bromiley and T. F. Torrance, vol. 3.3, Study Edition 18 (London: T & T Clark, 2010), 239. (Italics added.)

10. Raymond Gillespie, "Imagining Angels in Early Modern Ireland," in *Angels in the Early Modern World,* ed. Peter Marshall and Alexandra Walsham (Cambridge, UK: Cambridge University Press, 2006), 225.

Chapter 3: Three Reasons Why So Many of Us Believe in Angels

1. Michael Rogness, "A Fascination with Angels," *Word & World* 18 (1998): 58.
2. Eugene Peterson, "Writers and Angels: Witnesses to Transcendence," *Theology Today 51* (1994): 394–404.
3. Martin Israel, *Angels: Messengers of Grace* (London: SPCK, 1995), 23.
4. Israel, *Angels: Messengers of Grace,* 35.
5. Frederick Buechner, *Beyond Words: Daily Readings in the ABC's of Faith* (New York: HarperCollins, 2004), 17–18.
6. Karl Barth, *Church Dogmatics: The Doctrine of Creation,* ed. Geoffrey W. Bromiley and T. F. Torrance, vol. 3.3, Study Edition 18 (London: T & T Clark, 2010), 239.
7. As told in Eric Metaxas, *Miracles: What They Are, Why They Happen, and How They Can Change Your Life* (New York: Dutton, 2014), 239–40.
8. Emma Heathcote-James, *Seeing Angels* (London: John Blake, 2001), 19–20. Heathcote-James seems to hold out on whether they were angels or not.
9. David Keck, *Angels and Angelology in the Middle Ages* (New York: Oxford University Press, 1998), 142.
10. Peter Marshall and Alexandra Walsham, "Migrations of Angels in the Early Modern World," in *Angels in the Early Modern World,* ed. Peter Marshall and Alexandra Walsham (Cambridge, UK: Cambridge University Press, 2006), 23.
11. Peter J. Kreeft, *Angels and Demons: What Do We Really Know About Them?* (San Francisco: Ignatius, 1995), 72.

Chapter 4: The Four Most Important Words About Angels

1. Karl Barth, *Church Dogmatics: The Doctrine of Creation,* ed. Geoffrey W. Bromiley and T.F. Torrance, vol. 3.3, Study Edition 18 (London: T & T Clark, 2010), 82.
2. Barth, *Church Dogmatics: The Doctrine of Creation,* 173.

3. Joel J. Miller, *Lifted by Angels: The Presence and Power of Our Heavenly Guides and Guardians* (Nashville: Thomas Nelson, 2012), 25.

4. Miller, *Lifted by Angels,* 19–21.

5. Angels that don't summon us to God are called, in the Bible, "demons" or "unclean spirits" or the "principalities and powers." If belief in God entails belief in angels, belief in angels entails belief in anti-God spirits called demons.

6. Andy Angel, *Angels: Ancient Whispers of Another World* (Eugene: Wipf & Stock, 2012), 37–38. I have reformatted this material into a list, and I have added italics to draw our attention to the key actions of angels.

7. Jean Daniélou, *The Angels and Their Mission According to the Fathers of the Church,* trans. David Heimann (Westminster, MD: Newman, 1957), 34–43.

Chapter 5: Angels Express God's Love

1. Jonathan Macy, *In the Shadow of His Wings: The Pastoral Ministry of Angels Yesterday, Today, and for Heaven* (Cambridge, UK: Lutterworth, 2011), 4. Very few have written about the spiritual value of angels. Besides Macy and me, one of the few who has is T. F. Torrance, and he finds five elements in their spiritual value: (1) revelation, (2) worship, (3) providence, (4) participation in the future, and (5) mission. See Torrance, "Spiritual Relevance."

2. Wesley Hill, *Spiritual Friendship: Finding Love in the Church as a Celibate Gay Christian* (Grand Rapids, MI: Brazos, 2015), 42, with endnote.

3. Martha Sterne, *Alive and Loose in the Ordinary: Stories of the Incarnation* (Harrisburg, PA: Morehouse, 2006), 54.

Chapter 6: Angels Confirm God's Presence

1. The terminology used here is confusing to many. One way to make sense of the confusion is by saying, in truth, that God is manifest here in various ways.

2. Stephen F. Noll, *Angels of Light, Powers of Darkness: Thinking Biblically About Angels, Satan and Principalities* (Downers Grove, IL: InterVarsity, 1998), 162. If one compares 2 Kings 2:11–12, where Elijah is translated into heaven with horses

and chariots of fire, with Psalm 68:17, which says God is accompanied by thousands of chariots, and then also Zechariah 6:1–7, where the chariots are "spirits" (angel-like beings) sent by God, we are reasonably convinced the chariots and horses of our Elisha story are angelic messengers.

3. Peter J. Kreeft, *Angels and Demons: What Do We Really Know about Them?* (San Francisco: Ignatius, 1995), 83.

Chapter 7: Angels Sent to Redeem

1. In Exodus 25:17–22 they protect the "atonement cover" in the tabernacle; in 1 Kings 8:6-7 they do largely the same for the ark.
2. Bill T. Arnold, *Genesis,* New Cambridge Bible Commentary (New York: Cambridge University Press, 2009), 72.
3. A *lamb* in English refers to a young sheep, while *ram* refers to an adult male sheep. The Hebrew for *lamb* in Genesis 22:8 is a generic term for a sheep or a goat.

Chapter 8: Angels Teach from the Beginning

1. Bruce Gordon, "The Renaissance Angel," in *Angels in the Early Modern World,* ed. Peter Marshall and Alexandra Walsham (Cambridge, UK: Cambridge University Press, 2006), 63.
2. Karl Barth, *Church Dogmatics: The Doctrine of Creation,* ed. Geoffrey W. Bromiley and T. F. Torrance, vol. 3.3, Study Edition 18 (London: T & T Clark, 2010), 210.
3. Tracy K. Smith, *Ordinary Light: A Memoir* (New York: Alfred A. Knopf, 2015), 318.
4. David Albert Jones, *Angels: A Very Short Introduction* (Oxford: Oxford University Press, 2011), 7.

Chapter 9: Angels Teach the Bible's Big Ideas

1. G. B. Caird, *New Testament Theology,* ed. L. D. Hurst (Oxford: Clarendon, 1994), 380.

2. What, then, is the distinction between what angels do here and what the Spirit does? The answer is "We can't be sure." But this is how I see it. At times God the Spirit sends angels to do what at other times the Bible says the Spirit does. Either way, it is the work of God the Spirit, whether done directly or indirectly through angels.

Chapter 10: Angels Bring God's Comfort

1. Valery Rees, *From Gabriel to Lucifer: A Cultural History of Angels* (London: I. B. Tauris, 2012), 57.
2. Other terms for "bad" angels are "demons" or the "principalities and powers."
3. Marilyn Chandler McEntyre, *A Faithful Farewell: Living Your Last Chapter with Love* (Grand Rapids, MI: Eerdmans, 2015), 113–14.

Chapter 11: Angels as God's Very Presence

1. See M. F. Rooker, "Theophany," in *Dictionary of the Old Testament: Pentateuch,* ed. T. Desmond Alexander and D. W. Baker (Downers Grove, IL: InterVarsity, 2003), 863–64. For a more scholarly study, see Stephen L. White, "Angel of the Lord: Messenger or Euphemism?," *Tyndale Bulletin* 50 (1999): 299–305.

Chapter 12: Guidance Angels

1. C. S. Lewis, *The Screwtape Letters* (New York: HarperOne, 2001), 4, 24, 31, 38.
2. For a wonderful sketch of these journeys, see Valery Rees, *From Gabriel to Lucifer: A Cultural History of Angels* (London: I. B. Tauris, 2013), 153–194.
3. Kathleen Norris, *Amazing Grace: A Vocabulary of Faith* (New York: Riverhead Books, 1999), 328.

Chapter 13: Advocate Angels

1. This story was told to me via personal correspondence.

Chapter 14: Guardian Angels

1. U. S. Catholic Church, *The Catechism of the Catholic Church* (New York: Doubleday, 1995), 98 (section 336).

2. Valery Rees, *From Gabriel to Lucifer: A Cultural History of Angels* (London: I. B. Tauris, 2012), 172.

3. Martin Israel, *Angels: Messengers of Grace* (London: SPCK, 1995), 37.

4. Martin Luther, *Lectures on the Minor Prophets III: Zechariah,* ed. Hilton C. Oswald, Luther's Works 20 (St. Louis: Concordia, 1973), 171.

5. Trevor Johnson, "Guardian Angels and the Society of Jesus," in *Angels in the Early Modern World,* ed. Peter Marshall and Alexandra Walsham (Cambridge, UK: Cambridge University Press, 2006), 191–213, here 193.

6. Johnson, "Guardian Angels and the Society of Jesus," 211. For another translation, see www.preces-latinae.org/thesaurus/Basics/AngeleDei.html. Hence: "Angel of God, my guardian dear, to whom God's love commits me here, ever this day (or night), be at my side, to light and guard, to rule and guide. Amen."

7. Johnson, "Guardian Angels and the Society of Jesus," 212.

8. John Calvin, *Institutes of the Christian Religion,* ed. John T. McNeil, trans. Ford Lewis Battles, The Library of Christian Classics 20–21 (Philadelphia: Westminster John Knox, 1960), 167 (1.14.7).

9. Joel J. Miller, *Lifted by Angels: The Presence and Power of Our Heavenly Guides and Guardians* (Nashville: Thomas Nelson, 2012), 100.

10. Charles R. Jaekle, *Angels: Their Mission and Message* (Harrisburg, PA : Morehouse, 1995), 15–16.

11. Jonathan Macy, *In the Shadow of His Wings: The Pastoral Ministry of Angels Yesterday, Today, and for Heaven* (Cambridge, UK: Lutterworth, 2011), 98.

Chapter 15: Announcement Angels

1. Stephen F. Noll, *Angels of Light, Powers of Darkness: Thinking Biblically About Angels, Satan and Principalities* (Downers Grove, IL: InterVarsity, 1998), 173.

2. He cites the early fathers of the church, Origen and Eusebius.

3. Martin Israel, *Angels: Messengers of Grace* (London: SPCK, 1995), 8.

Chapter 16: Temptation Angels

1. Jonathan Macy, *In the Shadow of His Wings: The Pastoral Ministry of Angels Yesterday, Today, and for Heaven* (Cambridge, UK: Lutterworth, 2011), 61.

Chapter 17: Big-Event Angels

1. T. F. Torrance, "The Spiritual Relevance of Angels," in *Alive to God: Studies in Spirituality Presented to James Houston* (Downers Grove: InterVarsity, 1992), 136–137.

2. Emma Heathcote-James, *Seeing Angels* (London: John Blake, 2001), 33, with discussion on 32–44. The percentages in what follows are rounded to their approximate.

Chapter 18: Warrior Angels

1. Jean Daniélou, *The Angels and Their Mission According to the Fathers of the Church,* trans. David Heimann (Westminster, MD: Newman Press, 1957), 45–46.

2. The Episcopal Church, *The Book of Common Prayer* (New York: Oxford University Press, 1990), 193.

3. Todd Lighty, et al. "Chicago's Flawed System for Investigating Police Shootings," *Chicago Tribune,* December 5, 2015, www.chicagotribune.com/news/watchdog /ct-chicago-police-accountability-20151204-story.html.

4. For text, translation and commentary, see Paul F. Bradshaw, Maxwell E. Johnson, and L. Edward Phillips, *The Apostolic Tradition,* Hermeneia (Minneapolis: Fortress, 2002).

5. *The Apostolic Tradition,* 21.

6. *The Catechetical Lectures of S. Cyril, Archbishop of Jerusalem,* rev. ed., Edwin Hamilton Gifford, D.D., in *Nicene and Post-Nicene Fathers of the Christian Church,* vol. 7, second series (Grand Rapids, MI: Wm. B. Eerdmans, 1893).

Chapter 19: Angels Judge

1. Jane Williams, *Angels* (Grand Rapids, MI: Baker Books, 2007), 21.

2. Philip M. Soergel, "Luther on the Angels," in *Angels in the Early Modern World,* ed. Peter Marshall, and Alexandra Walsham (Cambridge, UK: Cambridge University Press, 2006), 64–82, the story is summarized on 64. Another summary can be found in Jürgen Beyer, "On the Transformation of Apparition Stories in Scandinavia and Germany, c 1350–1700," *Folklore* 110 (1999): 42.

Chapter 20: Angels Liberate

1. Billy Graham, *Angels* (Nashville: Thomas Nelson, 1995), 14–15.

2. Marilynne Robinson, *Gilead* (New York: Farrar, Straus and Giroux, 2004), 38–39.

3. Alexandra Walsham, "Angels and Idols in England's Long Reformation," in *Angels in the Early Modern World,* ed. Peter Marshall and Alexandra Walsham (Cambridge, UK: Cambridge University Press, 2006), 134–67. Google "St. Mary Abchurch dome London" to see images of the angels praising God, here represented in Hebrew letters.

4. Elizabeth Reis, "Otherworldly Visions: Angels, Devils and Gender in Puritan New England," in *Angels in the Early Modern World,* ed. Peter Marshall and Alexandra Walsham (Cambridge, UK: Cambridge University Press, 2006), 282–296, quoting 282.

Chapter 21: Angels Send on Mission

1. Christopher J. H. Wright, *The Mission of God: Unlocking the Bible's Grand Narrative* (Downers Grove, IL: InterVarsity, 2006), 264 (but see 252–264). Wright is leader of the Cape Town Lausanne Congress.

2. This story was told me via personal correspondence.

3. I have written about this in Scot McKnight, *The Heaven Promise: Engaging the Bible's Truth About Life to Come* (Colorado Springs: WaterBrook, 2015).

4. In Jean Daniélou, *The Angels and Their Mission According to the Fathers of the Church,* trans. David Heimann (Westminster, MD: Newman Press, 1957), 58. The original can be found at Origen, *Homilies on Luke,* The Fathers of the Church Series (Washington, DC: Catholic University Press of America, 1996), 54. Not all agree, and a listing of interpretive possibilities is found in Everett Ferguson, "Angels of the Churches in Revelation 1–3: Status Questionis and Another Proposal," *Bulletin for Biblical Research* 21 (2011): 371–86.

Chapter 22: Angels Intercede

1. Uriel, Raphael, Raguel, Michael, Saraqa'el, Gabriel, and Remiel. See 1 Enoch 20:2-8.

Chapter 23: Angels Lead in Worship

1. David Albert Jones, *Angels: A Very Short Introduction* (Oxford: Oxford University Press, 2011), 85.

2. Andrew Bandstra has investigated whether the Bible says angels "sing," and while he has some hesitations he has concluded that the angels praise God in song. See Andrew Bandstra, *In the Company of Angels: What the Bible Teaches, What You Need to Know* (Ann Arbor, MI: Vine Books/Servant Publications, 1995), 54–56.

3. T .F. Torrance, "The Spiritual Relevance of Angels," in *Alive to God: Studies in Spirituality Presented to James Houston* (Downers Grove, IL: InterVarsity, 1992), 131 (italics added).

4. This quotation from Temple is found in S. Christou, *Informed Worship* (Cambridge: UK, 2009), 14.

5. That is, to 4Q405, fragment 20, lines 7-14. Translation from Florentino García Martínez and Eibert J.C. Tigchelaar, eds., *The Dead Sea Scrolls Study Edition,* 2 vols. (Grand Rapids, MI: Eerdmans, 1997). All textual notations have been removed for clarity.

6. Andrew B. McGowan, *Ancient Christian Worship: Early Church Practices in Social, Historical, and Theological Perspective* (Grand Rapids, MI: Baker Academic, 2014), 121.

7. J. R. R. Tolkien, *The Silmarillion* (2d ed.; New York: Ballantine, 1999), 3–12.

8. Walter C. Smith, author.

9. The idea of vertigo comes from Robert Louis Wilken, "With Angels and Archangels," *Pro Ecclesia* 10 (2001): 460–474, here 474. www.the-highway.com/forum/ubbthreads.php/posts/44959/Worship_-_Robert_Louis_Wilken.html

Appendix: The So-Called Hierarchy of Angels

1. Pseudo-Dionysius, *The Complete Works,* trans. Colm Luibheid, The Classics of Western Spirituality (Mahwah, NJ: Paulist Press, 1987), 143–91.

2. For an extensive scholarly discussion of various cosmologies that include angels and demons, see Valery Rees, *From Gabriel to Lucifer: A Cultural History of Angels* (London: I. B. Tauris, 2013), 19–53.

3. The apostle Paul says he was caught up to the "third" heaven, which corresponds then to this highest (first) choir or order of angels; 2 Corinthians 12:2.

4. Dante connected a planet with each member of the three choirs, added a level and connected the four virtues with each of the levels. Marsilio Ficino connected each level to contemplating the three persons of the Trinity. See Valery Rees, *From Gabriel to Lucifer: A Cultural History of Angels* (London: I. B. Tauris, 2013), 45, for a quotation summary. All of this is both speculative and interesting to specialists.

5. 1 Enoch 20:1-8. Translation from James H. Charlesworth, ed., *The Old Testament Pseudepigrapha,* 2 vols. (Garden City, NY: Doubleday, 1983).

6. This is found in *Avot Rabbi Nathan* 43.7. See *The Sayings of the Fathers,* trans. Judah Goldin, Yale Judaica Series (New Haven: Yale University Press, 1990).

7. Found in *Hilchot Yesodei ha Torah,* II, 7. See *Mishneh Torah* online at: www.chabad.org/library/article_cdo/aid/904962/jewish/Yesodei-haTorah-Chapter-Two.htm/.

8. Valery Rees, *From Gabriel to Lucifer: A Cultural History of Angels* (London: I. B. Tauris, 2013), 60.

9. Karl Barth, *Church Dogmatics: The Doctrine of Creation,* ed. Geoffrey W. Bromiley and T. F. Torrance, vol. 3.3, Study Edition 18 (London: T & T Clark, 2010), 96.

10. Barth, *Church Dogmatics: The Doctrine of Creation,* 79.

11. John Calvin, *Institutes of the Christian Religion,* ed. John T. McNeill, trans. Ford Lewis Battles, The Library of Christian Classics 20–21 (Philadelphia: Westminster, 1960), 169 (1.14.8).

12. Calvin, *Institutes of the Christian Religion,* 164 (1.14.4).

13. The Episcopal Church, *The Book of Common Prayer* (New York: Oxford University Press, 1990), 184.